INSURRECTIONARY INFRASTRUCTURES

BEFORE YOU START TO READ THIS BOOK, take this moment to think about making a donation to punctum books, an independent non-profit press,

@ https://punctumbooks.com/support/

If you're reading the e-book, you can click on the image below to go directly to our donations site. Any amount, no matter the size, is appreciated and will help us to keep our ship of fools afloat. Contributions from dedicated readers will also help us to keep our commons open and to cultivate new work that can't find a welcoming port elsewhere. Our adventure is not possible without your support.
Vive la open-access.

Fig. 1. Hieronymus Bosch, *Ship of Fools* (1490–1500)

First published in 2018 by punctum books, Earth, Milky Way.
https://punctumbooks.com

ISBN-13: 978-1-947447-42-4 (print)
ISBN-13: 978-1-947447-43-1 (ePDF)

LCCN: 2018940293
Library of Congress Cataloging Data is available from the Library of Congress

Book design: Vincent W.J. van Gerven Oei

HIC SVNT MONSTRA

INSURRECTIONARY

INFRASTRUCTURES

JEFF SHANTZ

Ⓟ

Dedicated to Eva Ureta
Breaking their windows and building our infrastructures

CONTENTS

INTRODUCTION

THERE HAS ALWAYS been resistance to capitalism. The nature and type of resistance shifts and changes as economic and political contexts change and as the balance of forces shift in and through struggle. Certain historic movements heighten or intensify struggle and resistance (as in the revolutions of 1848 and 1917 to 1919 or the rise of fascism in the 1930s). In these moments the learning curve changes, often dramatically, quickly, and questions of some importance take on greater, unavoidable, urgency. In such moments the oppositional choice posed famously as the choice between socialism or barbarism can come into sharp relief. At these times questions of the character of resistance and struggle sharpen.

For many, the current period of rising white nationalism, racist xenophobia, right-wing populism, and proto-fascism, which in the United States has thrown up the election of Trump (and ascendance of Trumpism and the so-called alt-right as the new expression of old racist nationalism) and which elsewhere has taken on the figure of Marine LePen (France) and calls for racist "values tests" for migrants (Canada), is such an intensified moment.

The imperatives and necessities of struggle crystallize and it becomes essential to be clearsighted, strategically and tactically sound, about positive ways forward (away from barbarism and

13

toward something we might call socialism, communism, anarchism). Questions of organizing and the organized balance of forces matter. So too do questions of how a non-military majority can opposes a system protected by military forces at all levels, from municipal police to imperialist armies. Our strength is in numbers but we remain isolated and divided, reflecting atomized life in a capitalist market in which survival is a matter of personal pursuit.

For some there is a stasis, a replaying of familiar protests forms like demonstrations, street marches, rallies, only now with attempts and some successes in building them on a larger scale. This is exemplified in the Women's March and other protests such as the "Not My President" demonstrations mobilized around and after the Trump inauguration.

For many, coming from more radical perspectives, particularly some anarchists, there is a manifestation of an understandable growth in (an already existing) impatience. This is the righteous desire for insurrection — for fire to the existing social structures — now. The allure of insurrection has had a hold on many anarchists well before the rise of Trump and is really an expression of a proper disgust with, hatred of, statism and capitalism and a recognition that every day the system inflicts unbearable harm on people. In a very real sense we cannot wait. Yet this desire finds expression in a response fueled as much by hopefulness, wishful thinking, as by an accurate assessment of the situation — the balance of forces, the fields of power, the distribution of resources, capacities for success, prospects for victory.

One thing that is certain is that the events of 2015 to 2017 in North America in particular have spurred people from various anti-capitalist perspectives to turn renewed attention and focus to issues of organization and the pressing need for building resources to sustain and expand struggles in a context in which the forces of reaction have organized and mobilized — and whose organizing and mobilizing are expanding apace, with vigor and violence. The time for protest and dissent has long ago passed. Hopefulness and angry desire, while satisfying in various ways, are insufficient and misleading. The stakes seem to have been raised. The consequences of mistakes perhaps more severe. Though this cannot mean inaction or paralysis. The types of actions we engage in matter.

CRISIS

Capitalism is a social system founded in and developed through crisis. Crisis is the ongoing, regular feature of capitalist societies, the condition of life for most people. Economic crisis, political crisis, environmental crisis, cultural crisis, etc. This is not surprising given that capitalism is a system of organized violent dispossession geared toward, dependent upon, the continued expansion of violent dispossession.

A large part of this crisis is the separation of human communities from the means of subsistence. This is what the enclosures of the commons that kickstarted the development of capitalism in the 1600s and spread violently globally through systems of colonialism and imperialism have been all about. This has the dual effect of separating people from their communal and collective capacities to sustain themselves (from infrastructures and resources of life) and of making people depended on the capitalist labor market, and sale of their labor power to capital as *the* basis for survival (get a job or go hungry and homeless). The separation of people and their communities from necessary resources and infrastructures of life ensures recurring crises as a permanent feature of life for the majority of the global population.

At the same time specific state regimes wield special and particular powers to create and manage crisis within communities of exploited and oppressed people. Through policy and programs they can target communities for crisis and the breaking of budding opposition or resistance. The period of neoliberal capitalism has been a period of state management of the working class through constructed crisis (strategic creation of crisis). The state under neoliberalism is a form of what I have called, following autonomist Marxist Antonio Negri, a Crisis State, geared toward manufacturing the precarity and desperation of the working class, particularly but not exclusively along racialized lines (see Shantz 2016). This is distinct from the forms of welfare state managerialism and incorporation of the working class as a mechanism for defusing class conflict. The Crisis State is social war laid bare.

The Trump regime has been a Crisis State *par excellence* as it wields executive orders targeting specific, especially vulnerable, sectors of the working class for demonization and punishment. And while some have mistakenly posed the Trump administration as chaotic and disorderly, there is reason to believe that it is acting tactically and strategically to effect crisis among opponents and to achieve its own interests as representatives of the building wing of capital, what administration leaders like Steve Bannon refer to as "economic nationalism." Disorientation and disruption are the Trump administration's *modus operandi,* not mistakes or incompetence — it is, in fact, their competence.

The Trump White House fully intended to cause panic and desperation with the immigration ban executive order. This is a classic Crisis State move to destabilize, divide, confuse, and pressure working class communities. It is geared toward a reactive politics, a politics of desperate response. According to an article in *Bloomberg Businessweek* Trump strategist Steve Bannon arranged the timing of the order specifically for a Friday afternoon with no warning. Bannon expected that Trump opponents, off work over the weekend, would stage public protests. This is what he wanted according to *Bloomberg* and it happened. Quoting a senior administration official, the idea was that the large scale but symbolic protests would do little against the ban but would galvanize Trump supporters and rally them around the delivery of a campaign promise in the face of "liberal" opposition.

By releasing reactionary executive order after reactionary executive order the Trump White House is strategically sowing crisis among the working class and oppressed, particularly, of course, among racialized communities. The effect is to keep opposition constantly reeling, constantly reacting after the fact.

And to elicit some form of unrest — but on the familiar terrain of dissent or anger rather than organization and alternative. It keeps opposition busy responding — not proactively building. It also dissipates strategic development and tactical action, in the cause of responding to crises that seem, and often are, pressing.

The capacity of states and capital to bring working class communities to crisis, both chronic and acute, has been largely uncontested at least in meaningful and durable ways throughout the neoliberal period. The Trump regime has extended the scope and perhaps rapidity of Crisis State deployments significantly. It is an open form of rule by crisis.

So now as much as ever the need to build social infrastructures that can withstand and overcome crisis while also posing the possibility of bringing the Crisis State itself to crisis is of vital importance. As the building wing of capital advances its own projects we need to develop ours.

AN AGE OF INFRASTRUCTURE

In many ways this is a period of infrastructure and logistics. And of intense struggles over infrastructure and logistics. Industrial capital and the neoliberal state are simultaneously expanding through infrastructure development projects. This is particularly true as it relates to extreme energy projects in the last gasp of the fossil fuel economy. We see this in terms of tar sands developments, fracking, pipeline construction, dams, railway building, highways, and port expansion. To get at extreme energy and get it to market and to fuel industrial production.

In many ways President Trump represents the infrastructure wing, the building wing of capital. And his commitments and priorities have been, in addition to pipelines, coal, fossil fuels generally, to development of so-called Brownshirt (repressive) infrastructure (jails, prisons, detention centers, border walls, etc.). Note too his early proposal to expand military spending by 54 billion dollars even as the us faces massive war-driven debt.

Yet at the same time the forces that might oppose this — that speak perhaps too easily of insurrection — have minimal infrastructures, or experiences with their own infrastructures, with which to wage the battles they wish to. They have not even the bare minimum of self-defense infrastructure and resources to fend off attack from the more rabid Right, let alone from a mechanized military state that has shown in policing contexts across the US or colonial contexts like the assault on Standing Rock water defenders that it will readily deploy that force, and in lethal fashion, against its supposedly "own civilians," whether engaged in passive or "peaceful" protest or otherwise.

Happily, the response to the ban executive order was more than the familiar protests and showed that there are some important infrastructures potentially in formation. People mobilized and organized to stop deportations or provide legal support for people detained at airports. Churches (always ahead on building their own, if certainly not usually insurrectionary infrastructures) have rightly organized sanctuary networks for migrants. These are important examples.

ONWARD

This is a book about insurrection. About the passionate drive to end capitalism and the state that advances it. It is also a book about infrastructures. About building and sustaining the shared and collective resources needed to bring capital and states to the end they deserve. There can be no revolution without multiple insurrections. Insurrections are necessary but not sufficient components of revolution. For insurrections to play this part they must have bases in the needs, aspirations, desires of communities of the exploited and oppressed. And they must have foundations of resources — insurrectionary infrastructures.

This remains a call for insurrection, or, better yet, uprisings of the exploited and oppressed to be sure. But it is also a call for the serious building work, organizing work, that needs to be done if the first thought is to mean anything at all in real terms. Not as hope. Not as propaganda (of the deed or otherwise). There should be no illusion about what insurrection means or will bring. And there should be no illusions about what would be needed (at minimum) to have a chance of carrying it through. It is also necessary to recognize that activist insurrections (street battles, hard direct action, etc.) are not the same as peoples' uprisings and community riots, etc.

This is not to say that uprisings can or will be fully planned and organized ahead of time. Of course they will not be. Uprisings will happen as exploited and oppressed communities stand up and say "enough is enough." And activists and organizers, radicals of various types should do what they can and must support them as they can.

This is not a suggestion that people should wait for perfect conditions (that will never arrive) or delay collective expressions of anger until some mythical "time is right." Rather it is to recognize that when uprisings do occur already existing infrastructures are necessary to defend them, sustain them, care for people, feed struggle, and finally move to an offensive movement rather than a defensive one. And we need to ask what resources we have to meet these needs. And how will we build them? It is even more important to do so precisely because circumstances will not be perfect or even ideal when uprisings do occur. More will be needed to give them a real fighting chance against a more powerful (or at least more weaponized) enemy.

Many insurrectionists are involved in infrastructure building and are diligent about it. Hopefully this will encourage that work. On the other hand it can be said that perhaps too many who are doing great work focused on infrastructure building can forget that the aim is uprising, overthrow. I have seen this in various contexts. Infrastructure should support the overthrow of the existing order and provide a basis for replacing it with something better — something that is ours — by us and for us. The idea is not to carve out some comfortable space to survive within the system as it persists.

Some infrastructures are clearly essential on an ongoing basis. Medical care resources, reliable food supplies, shelter, autonomous energy, self-defense resources, etc. Others will be pressed forward on an emergency basis. Sanctuary spaces and networks, a new underground railroad, safe houses. As syndicalists have long argued one of the best ways to secure these infrastructures is to organize the workers who already provide these resources (nurses, paramedics, and doctors, agricultural and food workers, alternative energy workers, construction workers, etc.). There is no need to recreate fully these infrastructures in shadow networks from scratch. But they are necessary.

Insurrectionary infrastructures are bases for autonomy and self-determination for communities of the exploited and oppressed, the working class. They are necessary for decent lives in the here and now of everyday life. They are crucial for movements and uprisings that could pose an alternative to the current systems of state-enforced capitalism.

The questions of building longer term infrastructures, of developing strategies and tactics, of insurrection, are not the same as the issue of militant mobilization to address immediate existential threats. People can, must, and will mobilize to confront fascists and white supremacists in the streets. Nazis should be collectively punched in the face wherever and whenever they appear. Cops and other authoritarian creeps should be chased off campus as the black blocs did to Milo and his sycophants in Berkeley.

In the present period the stakes have been raised for many. The challenges we face, however, are constant. The balance of forces matters as always.

REFERENCES

Green, Joshua. 2017. "Does Stephen Miller Speak for Trump? Or Vice Versa?" *Bloomberg Businessweek.* February 28. https://www.bloomberg.com/news/features/2017–02–28/ does-stephen-miller-speak-for-trump-or-vice-versa.Shantz, Jeff. 2016. *Crisis States: Governance, Resistance, and Precarious Capitalism.* Earth: punctum books.

TAKING IT OFF THE STREETS

1

FROM RITUAL TO RESISTANCE

THE OCCUPY MOBILIZATIONS of 2011 offered to many some hope for a renewal of popular movements and alternatives to state capitalist arrangements. Recent mobilizations against Trump, in the form of anti-inauguration protests, have offered similar hope for a renewal of oppositional movements. Yet, perhaps few recurring events show the great disparity that exists between activist subcultures and broader working class and poor communities in North America than the privileging of street protests and demonstrations within activist practices. There is a rote ritualism that gives street demos and public expressions of dissent priority over other strategies and tactics. Yet mass demos that bring together atomized individuals without a real base or infrastructures supporting the mobilizations have minimal real impact. As James Herod suggests:

> But opposition movements gravitate again and again to these kinds of actions. "Taking to the Streets," we call it. Yet we can't build a new social world in the streets. As long as we're only in the streets, whereas our opponents function through enduring organizations like governments, corporations, and police, we will always be on the receiving end of tear gas, pepper spray, and rubber bullets, and almost everywhere in

the world but North America or Europe, real bullets, napalm, poisons, and bombs. (2007, 3)

It seems highly likely, indeed almost certain, that the spectacular waves of alternative globalization struggles from the summit protests since Seattle in 1999 to the Occupy movements launched in 2011 to the Not My President protests against Trump, will lose momentum and subside or drift into reformism in the absence of building real connections and moving toward struggles for control in workplaces and neighborhoods. The realms of workplaces, neighborhoods, and households have largely been ignored or abandoned as sites of transformative struggle by current activist movements (Herod 2007). Workplace struggles, where they exist at all, are dominated by bureaucratic mainstream unions focused on bargaining compromises with employers. Household organizing has been largely overlooked by radical activists — apart from those who retreat into their own (privatized and detached) collective houses. Issues of mental health and wellbeing have been given too little attention in movements focused on economics and politics in a more traditional and limited fashion.

BUILDING INFRASTRUCTURES OF RESISTANCE

Anarchists recognize (or should) that struggles for a better world beyond state capitalism must occur on two simultaneous levels. They must be capable of defeating states and capital and they must, at the same time, provide infrastructures or foundations of the future society in the present day. Indeed, this latter process will be a fundamental part of the work of defeating states and capital.

Through infrastructures of resistance movements will build alternatives but, as importantly, have capacities to defend the new social formations. These infrastructures of resistance will directly confront state capitalist power. Thus they will need to be defended from often savage attack. The key impulse is to shift the terrain of anti-capitalist struggle from a defensive position — reacting to elite policies and practices or merely offering dissent — to an offensive one — contesting ruling structures and offering workable alternatives. Movements need to shift from a position of resistance to one of active transformation.

There is a pressing need to take decision-making out of government bureaucracies, parliament, and corporate suites and boardrooms, and relocate it in autonomous assemblies of working class and poor people. There is also a need to take activism out of the atypical realms of demonstrations and protests and root it in everyday contexts and the daily experiences of working class and poor people's social lives.

This would serve to meet practical needs — of shelter, education, health, and wellbeing — while also raising visions for broader alternatives and stoking the capacity to imagine or see new possibilities.

Building infrastructures of resistance will directly affect movements in practical and visionary ways. It will also challenge ruling elites by pushing them into reactive, rather than purely offensive, and confident, positions. Such infrastructures of resistance would shift possibilities for strategizing and mobilization. They might render demonstrations unnecessary by offering a base for refusing or countering institutions and practices of states and capital. At the same time, more than simply opposing authoritarian institutions we might develop our own means for living the lives we desire.

Transformation must focus on controlling means of reproduction as well as means of production. Focus on workers' control alone leaves communities unable to allocate resources effectively and efficiently to meet broader needs (social or ecological). At the same time, community control without control of means of production would be futile, a fantasy. Even more, leaving households as privatized realms would reinforce an unequal gender division of labor and reinforce the duality of public and private realms of which anarchists generally critical. At the very least, neighborhood assemblies will constantly lose people who need to move in search of employment in the absence of worker control of industry.

A new social world cannot be built from scratch. Nor does it need to be. The mutual aid relationships and already existing associations that people have organized around work and personal interests (clubs, groups, informal workplace networks, even subcultures) can provide possible resources. At the same time, many infrastructures are needed, even today, in working class and poor neighborhoods and households many workers have only loose informal connections in their workplaces. In apartment complexes, households can link up in direct assemblies to organize shared resources. Some might include cooking, maintenance, laundry, health care, education, birthing rooms, and recreational facilities.

Building infrastructures of resistance encourages novel ways of thinking about revolutionary transformation. Rather than the familiar form of street organization or protest action, within constructive anarchist approaches, the action is in the organizing. There need to be already existing infrastructures or else a radical or revolutionary transformation will be impossible (or disastrous). On the need for pre-existing revolutionary infrastructures, we might note similarly that even larger mobilizations such as general strikes cannot have a meaningful impact in the absence of infrastructures of resistance. Under general strike conditions essential goods and services would be absent. Water, energy, food, and medical services would not be available without alternative associations or capacities to occupy and run workplaces to meet human social needs. These sorts of takeover themselves require pre-existing infrastructures.

UNIONS

One of the infrastructures that requires a real alternative is the labor union, institutions that have been at the heart of working class (workplace and community) struggles but which have long been conservatizing forces. For most anarchists, unions have lost any emancipatory capacities they might have once held. Indeed, for many anarchists, unions were never geared toward emancipation from capitalism, apart from the examples posed by a few syndicalist unions such as the Industrial Workers of the World in North America or the Confédération Nacional de Trabajo (CNT).

In some ways the role of radical capacity of unions is a moot point since unionization rates have declined to minuscule proportions in industries in the United States and Canada. There is presently an eight percent unionization rate in non-governmental workplaces in the United States. It is likely that the union movement will not recover, at least in its previously understood and recognized forms. Of course, the point is in no way to rebuild unions, since why would we expect them to perform differently than they have under previous conditions. The point is to build the strength of rank-and-file working class movements within broad struggles.

So the door is wide open, the floor cleared for new forms of working class workplace association or organization. Yet, there have been only halting, experimental attempts to fill the void. Some have been false starts while others hold some promise. Those that are most promising suggest a coming together of rank and file activists and militants.

Unions manage the labor and wage relationship. They do not oppose it. They represent a bureaucratic structure outside of the workplace rather than a democratic free association of workers within it. In fact, mainstream unions often work to stamp out or disband such associations where they do emerge in workplaces and challenge management and ownership.

Unions were readily co-opted and indeed co-opted themselves to become little more than mid-level managers of the contract and a range of working conditions (around pay, hours, job descriptions, vacations). Unions became disciplinary agencies against the autonomous activities of the membership. They prevent or manage strikes, job actions, sabotage, and occupations. They mobilize against absenteeism. At the same time formal union structures, legitimized in law, have been only one of the workplace efforts pursued by working people historically.

There can be no meaningful workplace strike without some workplace organizing. Militant organizing in the workplace requires rank and file alternatives, such as flying squads, working groups, and direct action groups. Some of these alternatives have developed with varying degrees of success as I have discussed elsewhere (see Shantz 2009).

CONCLUSION

Anarchist organizers must radically shift the terrain of anticapitalist struggles, moving to new battlegrounds rather than staying in the streets of protest and the town squares of Occupy movements. For constructive anarchists there are three primary sites of struggle with which anarchists must be engaged. These are the neighborhoods, workplaces, and households (see Herod 2007). Successful organizing in these areas should provide means to defeat states and capital, while also making the new world in the present — rather than waiting for a post-capitalist future. This shift must involve offensive as well as defensive strategies.

Movements have too often, for too long, been caught up in defensive or reactive struggles — responding to pieces of harmful legislation or damaging public policy, or opposing specific corporate or government practices. Such pursuits have dominated the vision of movements and activists in the Global North. It has led to a staleness of approach that fails to inspire people while leading instead to frustration and demoralization as rote repetitions of rituals are played out in response to external decisions by others (rather than asserting internal or organic needs and desires of the people directly involved). Instead, movements need to affirm their own wishes and visions of a better world.

Even more, the rituals of street protest do little to actually challenge power or structure of inequality. Typically they simply serve to reinforce the notion that liberal democracies allow spaces for dissent and divergent views. One might question the amount of energy, resources, and time put into single issue campaigns, street demonstrations, and camps on public lands. As a former Right-wing Premier of Ontario once remarked dismissively, in the face of mass street demonstrations: "I don't do protests." And he didn't. His police forces did.

Yet spectacular ritual events like demonstrations, protests, and public occupations dominate activist imaginations and organizational visions. This demonstration fixation has hindered social movements in liberal democracies for generations. The present period offers some new and encouraging openings — windows of opportunity for radical perspectives and movements against and beyond states and capital. To take advantage of this moment it is necessary to take a hard look at the ingrained rituals that have come to dominate movements, particularly those holdovers from periods of lesser mobilization.

REFERENCES

Herod, James. 2007. *Getting Free: Creating and Association of Democratic Autonomous Neighborhoods.* Boston: Lucy Parsons Center.

Shantz, Jeff. 2009. "Anarchy at Work: Contemporary Anarchism and Unions." *WorkingUSA: The Journal of Labor and Society* 12(3): 71–85.

2

ANARCHIST LOGISTICS

SUSTAINING RESISTANCE BEYOND ACTIVISM AND INSURRECTION

SOCIAL RESISTANCE HAS reached a certain impasse, a conundrum even as states impose austerity as an extended regime of governance. In North America, movements still race from crisis (response) to crisis (response) while organizing occurs around rather narrow projects. The alternative globalization politics of the last two decades have posed the emergence of opposition arising spontaneously; society holds the seeds of its own downfall which simply need to sprout. Two perspectives have framed this understanding: an insurrectionist one that seeks a spark (a riot perhaps) to jumpstart the uprising (tapping into the pre-existing anger that is "out there") and; a prefigurative one that seeks to inspire people by showing them the "better way." Both of these are matched with movement based activities, routines of protest and dissent. Both are, and have been, ill-suited to the challenges posed by aggressively active, and well resourced, opponents.

Movement-based mobilization, activism, is not sufficient. There is a real difference between social movements and social mobilizations (spread more broadly throughout communities). There is a connection, though, yet current movements in North America at least are struggling to get past oppositional activism (movementism) toward resistance, social mobilization. There is a need to move from the public squares to the neighborhoods.

PREPARATION IS KEY

The broad appeal and support of movements comes, not through a proper perspective, recognizable "activism" or insurrectionary sparks, but through meeting needs and securing victories. Many who join movements do so out of the desire to find community or security, and to win tangible gains, rather than adherence to the specific principles espoused by the movements. Organized alternatives must, in part, be able to offer a sense of belonging and community. As the anarchist Paul Goodman insisted in the context of 1960s' mobilizations, clear functionalist solutions must be developed (2010; Shantz 2014). Health clinics, schools, clothing and food provision, and community facilities and youth recreation are some of the essential resources movements have effectively secured. Infrastructures of resistance provide a logistical base for building broad support. Many of these infrastructures were destroyed and/or demobilized following the state repression against the upsurge of the late 1960s and early 1970s. The "war on crime/war on drugs" played a part in this. As neighborhood infrastructures crumble in locales across North America today there is no shortage of places for us to start.

The emphasis on elites, experts, and professionals in advanced capitalist societies, and the dominance of administrative bureaucracies peopled by professionals discourages people from asserting their own capacities for decision making. People are conditioned to seek expert advice and opinion. This is seen in the popularity of daytime talk shows like *Oprah* and in the profusion of self-help literature in which experts tell people how to pursue basic life tasks. Critics such as sociologist Heidi Rimke note that this is also a form of governance or self-regulation in neoliberal political regimes of state capitalism (2016). As Goodman noted, this leaves people unprepared to taste freedom when opportunities arise (2010).

Once people see that establishment structures are unwilling or unable to meet basic needs — and alternatives become available — they will struggle to break from those structures. Authorities are aware of this and typically respond with repression in cases where this appears to be happening, even in the early stages. The example of the state response to Occupy movements in various cities is but one recent case in point.

As Sun Tzu suggested famously, battles are won or lost before they are even fought. Preparation is key. There must be a capacity to achieve tangible victories and material gains. People must see results and have reason to believe that their own organizing and active participation within social struggles will improve their lives in real and meaningful ways. Anarchists must be able to help people and their communities to develop capacities to provide for material needs that the state cannot, and does not want to, provide. The community survival programs organized by the Black Panther Party in cities throughout the us provide important examples of this.

Members of non-elite groups need opportunities to change how we interact with one another economically. Thus we require spaces and venues to practice being cooperative with one another, and extending forms of cooperation in which we are already engaged, rather than being compelled by economic circumstances to act in ways that are competitive, manipulative, "cut-throat," or "dog-eat-dog." These practices, and establishing spaces and venues to pursue and extend them, are part of processes of revolutionizing our values as well as our social relations. Much work will need to be done to overcome capitalist values of avarice and deceit.

This is not to speak for a certain type of organization. Affinity groups also offer an important counter-weight or bulwark against social tendencies to avoid responsibility in the pursuit of enjoyment. Affinity contributes to conditions that support and ethics of responsibility, accountability, and commitment. They are based on deep sentiments of trust, loyalty, duty, and reliability. In a sense they offer a close peer group — one that can exert a certain amount of "peer pressure" on members. They also, as importantly, fulfill human needs and desires for security and a sense of social power.

At the same time, small groups cannot, despite the best wishes of insurrectionists, provoke mass uprisings or "manufacture revolution," or construct the conditions that will lead to mass rebellion. There is a pressing need to develop and organize bases of logistical support that can mobilize, support, and sustain what might become revolutionary struggle rather than seeing discontent dissipate in ineffectual, but cathartic, insurrections or riots. Uprisings and rebellions can then be extended and given lengthier duration and more positively impactful outcomes.

INSURRECTION

Insurrectionist perspectives have gained a certain, vocal, popularity in some anarchist circles. Much of insurrectionary rhetoric echoes to a degree Che Guevara's foco theory of uprising fomented by a small group of dedicated revolutionaries. Yet such an approach is largely suicidal in an advanced capitalist urban context. Particularly in the absence of real infrastructures of resistance that could sustain broader collective movements and militant struggles.

Most people from "our social sector," the working class, cannot even shoot a handgun, let alone use real weaponry in any combat capacity that would inevitably be required in a real uprising. While most anti-capitalist activists, including the radical Left cannot shoot straight, Right wing militias and National Rifle Association members are lethally competent.

This should not be mistaken for an appeal to non-violence. The current society is structured in violence. The choice is not between violence and non-violence but, rather, about the balance of forces engaged in violence on either side. Violence, more than words, offers at least some sense of vindication. But daring acts of violence are counter-productive and serve largely to present the prevailing powers as "militarily invulnerable" in the words of political prisoner Rashid Johnson.

People respond positively to revolutionary ideals when they can see the realistic possibility of success. Where they fight and win their confidence and morale increase. Where they lose repeatedly their commitment wanes. Repeated losses condition people to believe they cannot win. It leads to defeatism and avoidance. When movements are not properly prepared to fight, they are easily put down by authorities. This, then, reinforces the belief that movements cannot win. Organizing without preparing for revolutionary self-defense against authorities is actually preparing people to be defeatist. Failure reinforces conditioned pessimism.

Insurrection (which inevitably raises issues of armed struggle) in an advanced capitalist context cannot operate without a mass base. Securing that base requires established and durable infrastructures of resistance. Guerrilla actions without a mass-based political movement are futile.

LOGISTICAL ANARCHY

It has been said that logistics determine strategy. For radical movements there is much logistical work to be done. Building infrastructures of resistance is about preparing a logistical capacity to expand struggles against states and capital. States and capital can sustain the effects of individual and disconnected acts of dissent or protest. They cannot tolerate the effects of an open class war.

As John Gerrassi notes with reference to the Black Panther Party:

As long as their militancy was directed against individual police forces, the struggle (end empire's reaction) was relatively mild. Huey Newton was framed on a manslaughter rap and various other Panthers were arrested, but once the Panthers began to lead a class war by confronting the whole system (for example the breakfast program which made two crucial points: white society cannot feed Black children; the Black revolution can), the harassment of the Panthers changed to attempted extermination: cops raided Panther offices in San Francisco, Los Angeles, Seattle, Denver, Chicago, New York, and other cities, killed twenty-eight Panthers by the end of 1969, jailed hundreds, and [wiped] out the whole leadership. (1971, 32)

Those who struggle against states and capital must be prepared to defend ourselves. To understand the nature of the state is to know that it will attack to kill when and where it feels a threat to its authority and power. Revolutionary mass struggle must be logistical as well as economic, political, and cultural. The absence of any of these factors leads to failure as the study of past revolutions suggests. Resisting cultural domination, a favored preoccupation of much of the late twentieth and early twenty-first century Left and alternative globalization movements, is no substitute for resisting economic, political, and military domination.

Even under the most brutal military powers of imperialism, resistance forces can succeed by building a secure base in the neighborhoods, among the working classes and oppressed. This is achieved through the establishment of economic programs that serve the needs of the population. These programs are what I call infrastructures of resistance. They include schools, health clinics, food distribution centers, and so on. The need for preparation and reliable infrastructures is pressing. So too are coordinated work and venues to bring together often isolated organizers.

As Paul Goodman has argued, programs — economic, political, cultural, logistical — are needed that can displace the state and capital rather than merely oppose. In his view the shift from program to protest among "activism" is doomed to lose (even in meeting local material needs). Many broader infrastructures are needed within the oppressed sections of the working class especially. It is not enough to engage in agitational work, as in periods of low struggle or demobilization perhaps. Insurrection without preparation, a solid base, is mere fantasy.

In the current context where social institutions have collapsed, as in Greece and Spain, they have been replaced in part by projects of popular mutual aid. The ground had been prepared in the building of infrastructures of resistance in periods before the mass uprisings (and offered a basis for those uprisings).

REFERENCES

Goodman, Paul. 2010. *Drawing the Line Once Again: Paul Goodman's Anarchist Writings.* Oakland: PM Press.

Rimke, Heidi. 2016. "Mental and Emotional Distress as a Social Justice Issue: Beyond Psychocentrism." *Studies in Social Justice* 10(1): 4–17.

Shantz, Jeff. 2014. "Seeds Beneath the Snow: The Sociological Anarchy of Paul Goodman, Colin Ward, and James C. Scott." *Contemporary Sociology* 43(4): 468–73.

THE TERM RIOT is popularly used to describe collective acts of rebellion, unrest, or disorder, usually involving instances of property damage or destruction and/or personal violence. Riots typically occur in public spaces, such as urban streets or town squares but they can also occur in closed spaces such as prisons. Riots are generally portrayed as uncoordinated, spontaneous, and disorganized, though much recent research suggests that riots can involve planning and often develop their own logic and forms of coordinated solidarity within the course of the riot. Riots erupt for various reasons and there are different types of riots depending on the primary focus of anger or reason for emergence. These include economic riots (such as those over food or housing), political riots (as those over government repression, conscription, or taxation), "race riots" (based on ethnic or cultural differences), or sports riots (those following team victories or losses or involving clashes between team supporters). Riots usually involve property damage directed at targets perceived to represent the cause of a grievance, such as multinational companies, stores, or government buildings. Targets vary depending on the cause or motivation of the riot.

Regardless of the primary cause of the riot it is generally acknowledged by analysts of riots that there is usually an economic or class aspect to riots. Typically economic privation or dissatisfaction plays onto riot eruptions. Some commentators (see Barnholden) suggest that in the socio-economic contexts of class divided societies, marked by economic and political inequalities, riots will be regular, and unavoidable, occurrences.

Sociologists, arguing from a social structural perspective, such as Emile Durkheim, suggest that activities like riots can serve as a social safety valve, allowing non-elites to release pent-up anger over social, economic, or political dissatisfaction in a limited way that does not threaten society more fundamentally. For such sociologists, riots are understandable occurrences within class divided and unequal societies and the eruption of riots can serve as a useful warning signal that changes need to occur in society before it faces a larger social upheaval or disruption. Without occasional outbursts, as in riots, social anger could lead to more thoroughgoing or radical eruptions.

ON THE STREETS: FORMS OF ACTION FROM DEMONSTRATIONS AND PROTESTS TO RIOTS

Political demonstrations occur for various reasons, including lack of access to political and/or economic decision-making channels, dissatisfaction with ruling elites or authorities, desire for social transformation or more simply to register dissent with ruling practices publicly.

Demonstrations can be directed toward radical, even revolutionary, ends such as the overthrow of a state or property owners, as in the revolutions in France and Russia that overthrew the feudal order of landed property and governance. They can also be more modest in character mobilized toward less dramatic ends, as when people seek social reforms or policy changes or simply seek to display publicly their disagreement with rulers or governments.

Demonstrations also take on a variety of forms. They can vary in terms of duration, intensity, range of activities involved, levels of organization, aggression, motivation, and composition of participants and supporting groups. They can involve participation from different backgrounds, often working class, peasantry, poor people, religious groups, ethnic and racial minorities, even disaffected members of elite groups.

Some demonstrations are relatively spontaneous, unplanned and brief. This can occur in immediate response to the passage of a particular piece of legislation or a court decision that is viewed as unsatisfactory. It can also occur where worker respond to notice of impending job loss or workplace closure. Most are planned and organized and address longer standing grievances, concerns or economic or political policies and practices.

Protests often reflect a gap between goals and opportunities or between expectations or hopes and people's means to achieve those goals. Protests and riots occur where there is a sense that social change cannot, or can no longer, be achieved through, discussion, debate, and democratic dialogue. Government or police responses that seek to prevent or crack down on public expressions of dissent will often intensify those expressions, giving rise to riots, violence, rebellion, even revolution.

Conventional political protests in the contemporary period in Western liberal democracies rarely involve acts of violence or property destruction. Direct action protests, which have become more prevalent in the period of globalization, do involve the targeting of specific corporations or symbols of corporate power, as in the attacks upon Starbucks coffee shops and Nike stores during the Seattle protests against the World Bank meetings in 1999.

Some demonstrations can be defused simply by providing a contained space in which they might occur. People can gather, blow off steam, feel a sense of empowerment or public engagement and then disperse.

In countries like Canada there have been more sports riots than political riots although these often overlap with political issues. Yet liberal democracies like the us have been marked by regular outbreaks of riot and insurrection. Some commentators suggest that this reflects the greater disparity of income and wealth in the US, its larger gap between very wealthy and very poor, and the sharper class and status divisions (including intersections of race and class and the racialization of poverty).

In liberal democratic polities riots become more regular occurrences during periods of broader social struggle when organized dissent is more common and social movements are more active. During the 1960s riots and public uprisings were rather frequent occurrences. These included explicitly political actions, spurred by reactions to police violence, such as the riots during the Democratic National Convention in Chicago in 1968 and the "Days of Rage" actions the following year in the same city. These riots, and the radical movements that developed partly as a result of the riots impacted US politics and have been credited with playing a part in the US withdrawal from Vietnam. There were also more spontaneous eruptions, which were also rooted in political frustrations, such as the riots following the assassination of Dr. Martin Luther King Jr. in 1968. In 1967 alone there were more than 150 riots in the US occurring in 128 cities.

In the US, many of the most notable and infamous riots have been so-called "race riots." Indeed the term race riot itself emerges in the context of the US during the late 1800s. Among the most damaging and notorious race riots in US history include: Memphis 1866; Springfield, Illinois 1901; East St. Louis 1917; Chicago 1919; Omaha 1919; Tulsa 1921; Detroit 1943; Los Angeles "Zoot Suit Riots" 1943; Detroit 1967; Newark 1967; Akron 1968. Initially the term race riot was used to refer to acts of mob violence initiated and carried out by numbers of the majority racial, ethnic, or cultural group against members (individually or collectively) of one or more minority group. By the 1960s the term had come to be applied in situations involving public eruptions of collective violence involving members of racial, ethnic, or cultural minority groups. While the popular term for such events, and the term used by governments, emphasizes racialized aspects of the riots, critics note that modern race riots almost always have economic causes. These include unemployment, job discrimination, inadequate housing, economic depression, or economic transition (as in times of war production).

In response to the riots of the mid 1960s, the US government launched various commissions to study causes of riots and urban violence. The Kerner Commission of 1968 concluded, controversially, that the primary precipitating factor in race riots of the 1960s was ongoing racism by members of the white majority. This included systemic racism within institutions of economic and political authority. Economic conditions caused deeply felt grievances within minority communities but anger was stoked into active aggression following an incident of racism, often including violence committed by a majority member against a minority member, which became amplified through rumor and public representation.

Riots have become more regular occurrences within liberal democracies with the rise of alternative globalization movements and protests. During the late twentieth and early twenty-first centuries, popular mobilizations against capitalist globalization have often been marked by direct actions and the targeting of corporate property, particularly the property of multinational corporations like Nike, Starbucks, and McDonalds, for damage. Of much focus within such protests have been the activities of so-called black bloc anarchists, activists dressed alike in black garb to avoid detection or identification by police. Police aggression, violent arrests, and the indiscriminate use of tear gas, pepper spray, and water cannons against political demonstrators, have sparked riots within urban centers in which meetings of global capital are taking place. Riots have erupted during protests against capitalist globalization, and following aggressive policing practices, most notably in Seattle during the meetings of the World Trade Organization (WTO) in 1999 and in Miami during negotiation meetings for the proposed Free Trade Area of the Americas (FTAA). In dealing with protesters during the Miami demonstrations police and security agencies have developed the so-called "Miami model" of policing alternative globalization demonstrations. The Miami model, which has been applied against citizens in subsequent meetings of global capital involves: establishment of joint, multi-agency command networks; mass purchase and deployment of, often new or experimental, surveillance equipment; use of psychological operations to discredit protesters; association of anarchists with terrorists or criminals; mass arrests and detentions in temporary facilities; disruption of activist media centers and housing spaces; preemptive arrests; use of non-lethal weaponry against protesters; establishment of militarized zones behind fences and barricades; and containment of masses of people on side streets or public squares for lengthy periods of time, followed by mass arrests. Critics suggest that these very practices contribute to the radicalization of demonstrations thereby increasing the likelihood of riotous activities.

For some commentators, particularly those influenced by Marxism, riots represent forms of "primitive" rebellion, important for mobilizing public dissatisfaction but incapable of effecting real, lasting social transformations. While expressions of class anger, riots lack the organizational forms, such as a party, that would focus and direct that anger over greater periods of duration. For anarchist commentators, who conceptually reject the necessity of political parties, riots are more properly understood as insurrectionary moments, potentially capable of sparking broader social unrest and raising critical consciousness against economic inequality or state repression. In any event, for anarchists, riots are necessary precursors to larger revolutionary actions and cannot be readily dismissed as "primitive."

ON SOCIAL CONTROL AND STATE VIOLENCE

The extensive and often militant social and political struggles of the 1960s impelled states to re-think methods of social control. The most common recommendations were an expansion of the numerical size of police forces and the militarization of police through provision of advanced technology, weapons and training. Key in the expansion of police power in the US was the LEAA (Law Enforcement Assistance Administration), which was organized to extend policing along national lines through new technologies and strategies. Due in part to LEAA policies, military technology and weaponry, originally developed for use in warfare, were developed throughout police departments in the US as police organization adopted a largely paramilitary character.

The first modern police forces in the US were developed in industrialized urban centers in the industrialized northeast. Their main emphasis was "maintaining urban order" in the face of class conflict as cities grew through waves of migrants seeking employment. Critical theorists ask whose order is being maintained and what does this order look like in terms of inequality, liberty, freedom or exploitation?

Policing of protests reinforces and extends unequal class structures in society by focusing on activities predominantly of the poor and working class rather than the activities of elites, such as corporate crime, pollution, ecological destruction or workplace injustice.

It is not coincidental that historically the most aggressive policing has occurred during demonstrations organized and participated in by working class and poor people and racialized minorities, including Indigenous people in the US and Canada. Only with the anti-war protests of the 1960s was such aggressive policing deployed against middle class or privileged students. During the alternative globalization protests of the twenty-first century aggressive policing has been directed at diverse groups, reflecting the plural composition of those movements, consisting of a range of participants acting together.

For critics, policing of demonstrations provides a mechanism for elites, those who control wealth and resources, to suppress attempts by non-elites to re-distribute wealth and resources. Such policing provides a powerful agency for maintaining inequalities of wealth and power in class societies. Policing of demonstrations reinforces existing unequal property rights and the limited political processes of parliamentary democracy as the preferred or privileged form of political expression. Forms of politics outside of such legitimized, and hierarchical channels, are treated as deviant, threatening or even criminal.

In American history numerous cases show that local business people have had influence, even control, over directing police against striking workers. Very early in their history police were deployed by capital to harass picket lines and break workers' strikes. The strikes were a response to exploitation and economic deprivation yet police were not deployed against employers to end such harmful conditions. Police strikebreaking protects the interests of industrialists. Such actions serve to break working class resistance to the power of capital. Use of police to break strikes also defines collective organizing and assembly by workers as a criminal, rather than economic or political, act.

State forces were formed to deal with striking workers. The Coal and Iron Police were created in Pennsylvania in 1866 to control striking coal and iron workers. In 1905 the state formed a state police agency for use in strikebreaking. These official state forces gave a legitimacy to strikebreaking that private security, which lacked state authorization as keepers of the public order, could not claim.

Strikebreaking and union busting has also been a function of private police and security, most notably reflected in the history of the Pinkerton agency.

Similarly the earliest forms of policing in the southern US involved so-called "slave patrols" dating back to 1712 in South Carolina. The function of these patrols was to maintain discipline over slaves and prevent slave riots. Black people caught violating any laws were summarily punished.

The transformation of urban police forces from community forces managed at local levels in towns and cities in America to militarized forces organized along national lines and standards related to changes during the 1960s in which "law and order" became a matter of national politics. Much of the impetus for this change came from the visible social conflict and protests of the 1960s, beginning with civil rights marches and boycotts and followed by anti-war movements and student protests. Social reaction as in the "War on Drugs" campaigns were explicitly launched to break Black Power movements and organizing of insurrectionary infrastructures in Black working class neighborhoods. The period of conflicts included the numerous urban uprisings and so-called "race riots" against racism in cities such as Detroit, Washington, DC, and the Watts area of Los Angeles. Reports of these movements focused on and emphasized dramatic manifestations of disorder rather than the underlying issues and views of activists themselves.

Images of the violent policing of civil rights marches, as under Bull Connor's forces in Birmingham, caused American society and foreign audiences to recoil, providing an impetus for others to join the movement and leading for calls for restraint on local police and transformations in the structure of society itself. These provided some of the most shocking and lasting images of the era. The use of police dogs and water cannons against non-violent protesters, consisting largely of regular citizens from the local community, rather than militant activists and organizers, shifted public opinion against police and southern governments and reinforced protesters' claims of injustice, racism, and inequality.

Protesters are presented by police as dangerous individuals who belong to fringe groups or are disaffected members of society and pose a threat to society's "normal" functioning or way of life. In some cases terms like "professional protesters," which has become a key trope of the Trump administration, are used to disparage organizers and suggest they are not raising legitimate concerns but rather acting out of self-interest. In Toronto, the former Chief of Police identified direct action anti-poverty groups as "terrorists" and attempted to make simple membership in the groups illegal. Focus on policing can serve to shift attention towards technical processes and tactics, rather than the pressing need to expand social justice and end inequalities.

Even with regard to looting in specific riots, most acts of looting and community violence were not random or "senseless" but in fact were directed at businesses that had histories of cheating or taking advantage of the local residents. Despite this the riots of the 1960s were used as justification for the militarization of policing in local areas.

A similar process has occurred in the context of alternative globalization demonstrations and calls for tighter security and policing of such demonstrations. Demands for greater democratization and equality have been met by conservative calls for a "moderation of democracy" and the use of police to stifle growing social movements. Part of that response has been the reconstruction of police forces and policing to maintain public order while limiting popular mobilization.

Critical theorists view policing of demonstrations as a manifestation of class struggle. Such theorists argue that policing emerges with nation states to protect the material and social interests of power-holders. Policing of protests emerges where power-holders seek to control and regulate other groups.

Police have, since the earliest days of modern policing, regularly been deployed to disperse striking workers and break up picket lines. Much research shows that during the nineteenth century many of the gatherings against which police were deployed that were identified as "riots" were actually simply gatherings of striking workers. Targeting of such "riots" was clearly more than an issue of public order. Rather the suppression of strikes offered examples of policing to benefit economic elites. Police strikebreaking under the guise of riot control was an effort to defeat working class resistance to employers.

In the era of globalization protests, police have moved from attempting to restrain protesters directly by using traditional means such as batons, riot squads, and pepper spray, which failed during the Seattle protests of 1999 and the demonstrations against the IMF and World Bank in 2000, to develop containment strategies prior to demonstrations occurring in events of global bodies such as the World Bank or WTO. During the protests against the Organization of American States (OAS) in Windsor, Ontario in 2000, a security fence closed off several city blocks around the convention center at which meetings were scheduled to take place. Official delegates were flown to the meeting site by helicopter from Detroit. Protesters who approached the fence were then peppersprayed. The fence, sealing off several city blocks around the convention site, re-appeared as a crowd control technique during the 2001 protests against the OAS in Quebec City. There, protesters were bombarded by thousands of canisters of tear gas over three days of demonstrations. Water cannons and rubber bullets were also deployed.

THE CONSCIENCE COLLECTIVE OF THE RIOT: BREAKING INHIBITIONS

Sociologists also note that riots are not typically the unorganized and incoherent events that they appear to be from the outside. Sociologists drawing upon Durkheim suggest that participants within crowds develop their own value and belief systems, which serve to order and legitimize their activities. Thus there emerges a *conscience collective,* or shared value system, of the crowd which can influence the emergence and/or direction of a riot. Notably, the invasion of the crowd by police or perceived outsiders can spark a defensive reaction contributing to riotous activities. Social regulation breaks down and new forms of sociation and collective sentiment among rioters emerge, supportive of even greater riotous activities.

The vast majority of people regularly conform to social norms or rules and social expectations or conventions. Notions of normalcy and morality are supported by various social, cultural, political and economic sanctions. Ongoing socialization engenders habitual responses to authority that favor deference, respect, and acquiescence. To break through layers of socialization requires significant shifts in perception and consciousness.

Given levels of injustice, corruption, exploitation, inequality, and oppression it is perhaps surprising that protest, rebellion, and resistance are not more regular features of social life. Even more curious is the relative infrequency of occurrences in which ordinary people challenge authorities and political or economic elites. Even fewer are those who directly resist the undertakings of governments in a forceful manner.

Given the inhibition experienced by people in violating even minor or insignificant social rules or conventions it is clear how difficult resisting the demands of the state might be. It requires courage, conviction and a sense of possibility or feasibility, purpose, or effect. One must overcome internal as well as external barriers to action.

States and ruling elites have a range of strategies, tactics, methods, and techniques to control, constrain, discourage, and defuse resistance or opposition from non-elites or citizens. Police have at various points, in dealing with demonstrations, played upon the moral inhibitions people feel in resisting state demands. In specific contexts, such as anti-poverty demonstrations in Toronto, Canada since at least 2003, police have approached elderly demonstrators and parents with younger children present, questioning their responsibility and judgment by virtue simply of their being present at a political demonstration. In addition, police have suggested that participants might be at risk of violence or physical harm. Even more, police have, as in Toronto, threatened parents with loss of children and the possible intervention of children's service agencies, if parents remained at the demonstration site with their children. A heavy response can deter people from participating in future demonstrations. Similarly, policing demonstrations can serve as a reminder of the activity and vigilance of authorities.

This *conscience collective* can express a strong "us versus them" sentiment in which protesters come to view opponents harshly as enemies to be contested and overcome. Interestingly, this "us versus them" sentiment is also a well researched, long recognized and commented upon characteristic of police subcultures. Thus harsh actions by police can initiate a cycle of escalation as each side reinforces "us versus them" sentiments, increasing solidarity and a sense of grievance both among protesters and police. Policing demonstrations can contribute to a sense of social cohesion and group identity on both sides.

Often it is the presence of mass and/or aggressive policing that spurs protesters to become more militant or aggressive themselves. It can play into the constitution or identification of "us versus them" sentiments in which police and protesters confront one another within openly oppositional stances.

Race riots are typically sparked by incidents involving police in a minority neighborhood. Usually there is a real or perceived misconduct or act of aggression by police in the area. In response to police the riot can escalate including dramatic actions such as gunfire, arson and violence. Police and military partake in the escalation of violence from their side. The Kerner Commission investigating race riots in the 1960s in the US noted that almost every such eruption in the US in the 1960s and 1970s was sparked by a specific act of police violence in communities that had suffered under such violence for generations.

Restrictive practices can lead to broader rebellion as larger sections of the citizenry become frustrated or indignant as a result of perceived restrictions on rights to assemble or freedom of expression. Rebellions involve armed opposition to ruling authorities and can give rise to revolutions, in which significant social and political change is effected.

REFERENCES

Ellsworth, Scott. 1992. *Death in a Promised Land: The Tulsa Race Riot of 1921*. Baton Rouge: Louisiana State University Press.

Hobsbawm, Eric. 1965. *Primitive Rebels: Studies in Archaic Forms of Social Movements in the 19th and 20th Centuries*. New York: W.W. Norton.

Lynch, Michael J. and Raymond Michalowski. 2006. *Primer in Radical Criminology: Critical Perspectives on Crime, Power and Identity*. Monsey: Criminal Justice Press.

Mackay, Charles. 1960. *Extraordinary Popular Delusions and the Madness of Crowds*. New York: Farrar, Straus, and Giroux.

Sugrue, Thomas J. 2005. *The Origins of the Urban Crisis: Race and Inequality in Postwar Detroit*. Princeton: Princeton University Press.

Shantz, Jeff. 2011. *Active Anarchy: Political Practice in Contemporary Movements*. Lanham: Lexington.

Tepperman, Lorne. 2006. *Deviance, Crime, and Control: Beyond the Straight and Narrow*. Don Mills: Oxford University Press.

Tuttle, William M. 1996. *Race Riot: Chicago in the Red Summer of 1919*. Urbana-Champaign: University of Illinois Press.

4

THE CALL FOR INSURRECTION

NSURRECTION CONTINUES TO hold a central place in the imagination of many activists, including, especially, many who identify as anarchists. Indeed, as mentioned above, there is a powerful insurrectionist tendency within contemporary anarchism.

Yet despite its potency in stoking feelings of exhilaration and emotional release, and the visual drama of insurrectionary imagery, insurrections have little hope of toppling state capitalist structures. As much as insurrectionary moments release feelings of righteous outrage — the scream against injustice and oppression — they typically provide the legitimizing cover to allow states and capital to unleash a torrent of moralistic condemnation and re-affirmations of bourgeois civility.

As recent riots in my current home area (Vancouver) attest, the response of the state to insurrectionary moments is overwhelmingly one of repression, surveillance, and a push for the self-regulation of working class populations. Following the Vancouver hockey riots of 2011, for example, working class people were pressured, cajoled, and encouraged to become snitches turning in anyone they might recognize from the copious riot footage that was publicized in numerous venues, public, private, and community-based.

The spread of surveillance cameras, the proliferation of individually held personal recording devices, and the disappointing willingness of "decent" citizens to turn their neighbors and co-workers in, as Vancouver has painfully shown, means that many participants in insurrectionary events will be easily apprehended and given often lengthy, and usually disproportionate sentences.

As I have written elsewhere (Shantz 2012), in the absence of relevant social contexts, and the engaged relationships with one's fellows, that would provide a basis for understanding and appreciating the necessity if insurrectionary actions, people are liable to respond in a reactive fashion taking up the socially normalized language of moral outrage or confusion over such acts.

ON INSURRECTIONISM

The notion of insurrection strikes a curious note in the current context of undeveloped resources and self-defense capacities among progressive activists, anarchists, communists, etc. It is even more questionable in a context in which the forces of reaction and nascent fascism are at least well armed and increasingly well organized.

To speak seriously of insurrection means to be able to deploy some capacity for combat. This includes the use of weaponry. This is unavoidable given the requirements of a real uprising in a context of already developed capacities of opponents of insurrectionary risings, including the armed Right wing militia groups. To talk of insurrection means that they will shoot. And you better be prepared, in certain contexts at least, to shoot back.

While they might never admit it, most advocates of insurrectionism are actually advancing a perspective that corresponds to Che Guevara's foco theory of uprising fomented by a small group of dedicated revolutionaries. This is impractical and dangerous in the current context of advanced capitalist urban environments. Particularly in a situation in which real, meaningful infrastructures of resistance are absent or underdeveloped.

Most anarchists in North America cannot shoot straight, though some are starting to learn since the Trump election, as especially in the wake of Charlottesville. Right wing militias and National Rifle Association members "are dangerously proficient" when it comes to weapons use (Johnson 2011, 87). At the same time Rashid Johnson argues that the class character of Right wing militias and survivalists suggests that some might be potential allies. They have an inchoate and confused opposition to monopoly capitalism. It is obscured by conspiracy theories, paranoia, and religious fundamentalism and clearly needs some ideological education. We might not want to put much stock in that, however.

Guerrilla actions without mass based political and economic organizing are futile. Armed struggle or insurrection in an advanced capitalist context cannot operate abstractly. Developing that base requires establishing infrastructures of resistance. The action is in the organizing.

THE RED HERRING OF VIOLENCE

Again, this is in no way to argue against so-called violence. State capitalism and settler colonialism are always already inherently violent. That is their founding and signal character. They are developed and structured through the violence of dispossession, displacement, occupation, and exploitation (of land and labor). On an ongoing basis. The everyday violence of police, security, and military maintain this system of accumulation through theft. Under state capitalist contexts, the absence of war is not the presence of peace (social war is the reality).

Questions of violence are questions of strategy or tactics if one accepts a need for revolt and revolution. As Friedrich Engels famously remarked, "A revolution is not a tea party." The question of violence is a subordinate one. More fundamental is the question of how an insurrectionary movement, or tendency, organizes itself and focuses its actions. Violence must be directed only toward resting economic and political control from the hands of the ruling classes that the masses of people might govern their own lives.

The "revolutionary nihilism" of characters like Nechaev, who have used the cover of anarchy to peddle anti-social and tactically impoverished violence, results from an improper assessment of class forces and the despair of those detached from working class social power. Notably a certain nihilism has become popular again among a younger generation of people harmed by capitalism and left with a familiar sense of "no future" but lacking connection to infrastructures and resources that would pose real possibilities for an alternative future. Pessimism, while understandable given the odds facing those seeking radical change, cannot provide a basis for revolutionary organizing. Failure to understand class forces in society leads to the path of mercenary activity or nihilism and the loss of revolutionary purpose. There is a tendency to glamorize violence without political discipline and education. These latter attributes come through day to day organizing rooted in community infrastructures.

Society is structured in violence. The choice is not between violence and non-violence but, rather, about the balance of forces engaged in violence on either side. Violence, more than words, offers at least some sense of vindication. But daring acts of violence are counter-productive and serve largely to present the prevailing powers as "militarily invulnerable" (Johnson 2011, 104).

COMMUNITY CONNECTIONS FOR INSURRECTION

Revolutionaries must be connected to communities of the working class and poor. As Johnson suggests: "Without mass support, there can be no mass movement; indeed our struggle is nothing if not mass-oriented, isolated from and against the people, we become warlords — no better than the enemy" (Johnson

2011, 107). And this connectedness will not develop magically through the supposedly liberating or educative acts of insurrection (without context or base).

This relates to the insurrectionary notion of propaganda of the deed and the assumption that inspiring acts will inspire action. The most effective propaganda is building a capacity to meet people's needs while advancing abilities to fight current systems of exploitation and oppression.

There is a recognition that experiences of social struggle and social conflict are central in the transformation of people's outlooks and understandings, as well as shifting how they relate to one another — in terms of solidarity and mutual aid. Many understand their social conditions as unfair, unjust — exploitative. They know they are being screwed over and they know it is wrong. There is more class consciousness among exploited and oppressed people than is often admitted. What is less common is a sense of what to do about it or a reasonable belief, let alone expectation, that there are achievable and meaningful alternatives. And part of this gap is a direct result of the absence — the decimation and decline — of insurrectionary infrastructures.

Class consciousness is something that develops through people's experiences in the real world of everyday struggles. It is not something produced by the Left or by radicals. It is something that can be informed and sustained in collective, shared infrastructures. In any event, consciousness is contradictory and there is no perfect consciousness needed or possible prior to action. This is a basic statement against idealist approaches.

The participation and enthusiasm of non-activist community members will be won only by "causing them to see and feel the material benefits and needs of revolutionary change" (Johnson 2011, 91). There must be tangible victories and material gains. People must see results and have reason to believe that organizing and active participation within social struggles *will* improve their lives in real and meaningful ways. The organizers must be able to help people and their communities to develop capacities to provide for material needs "which the enemy state cannot and will not provide" (Johnson 2011, 91).

The community survival programs organized by the Black Panther Party in cities throughout the US provide important examples of this. For Rashid Johnson this goes much farther:

> This is the how-to of building a secure mass base from and within which a People's Army can effectively operate, and from which the movement may draw workers and soldiers. (2011, 91)

Members of non-elite groups need opportunities to change how we interact with one another economically (Johnson 2011, 98). Thus we require spaces and venues to practice being cooperative with one another, and extending forms of cooperation in which we are already engaged, rather than being compelled by economic circumstances to act in ways that are competitive, deceitful, domineering, or vengeful. The cooperative practices, and establishing spaces and venues to pursue and extend them, are part of processes of revolutionizing our values as well as our social relations. Much work will need to be done to overcome capitalist values of avarice and deceit.

For people to respond positively, and they will, to revolutionary ideas, they need to see some realistic possibilities for success. Fighting and winning increases confidence and morale but also capacities to fight more. Losing conditions people to expect more losing. It contributes to defeatism and disappointment. And leads to defensiveness and avoidance. Victories are important and it is crucial to think seriously about how we can win meaningful victories.

When organizers are not prepared to fight, they are easily put down by authorities. This, then, reinforces the belief that movements cannot win. Organizing without preparing for revolutionary self-defense against authorities is actually preparing people to be defeatist. For Johnson: "People react when they see that resistance is possible" (Johnson 2011, 115).

Anti-capitalist organizers cannot proselytize in a vacuum. There must be clear functionalist solutions developed. Movements require "social service programs through which to materially reach the broad masses, showing them the need for struggle and giving them something to fight for" (Johnson 2011, 133). Anti-capitalist organizers must get their hands dirty in mass-based projects. They must organize people around meeting their own needs. It is not enough to engage in agitational work, as in periods of low struggle or demobilization perhaps. A critical analysis of capitalism and imperialism is not sufficient.

Broad mass appeal and support come through meeting needs and securing victories. Health clinics, schools, clothing and food provision, and community facilities and youth recreation are some of the necessary services that must be provided. In a sense there are no small victories. Even seemingly minor successes can represent important advances, particularly in building people's confidence and the sense that struggle is not a waste of time and energy. For many working class and poor people losing is a too regular experience. Losing at school, at work, with housing tribunals, or welfare offices leads to the expectation of failure and the acceptance of defeat. It can contribute to what psychologists identify as learned helplessness. Victories, even apparently small ones can break that sense of hopelessness or futility. I have witnessed numerous people transform, almost immediately, from anxious skeptics to committed militants through something as simple as winning a welfare case challenge or successfully standing up to a bad boss over a wage dispute or landlord over an eviction order.

Many who join movements do so out of the desire to find community or security rather than adherence to the specific principles espoused by the movements. Organized alternatives must, in part, be able to offer a sense of belonging and community. For Johnson: "People can be mobilized to support or at least be neutral toward, most any cause — even something as counterproductive as an open-air neighborhood drug market — if they're given a sense of objective benefit, security, and community" (Johnson 2011, 161). Once people see that establishment structures are unwilling or unable to meet basic needs — and alternatives become available — they will struggle to break from those structures.

Authorities are aware of this and typically respond with repression in cases where this appears to be happening, even in the early stages. The example of the state response to Occupy movements in various cities is but one recent case in point.

There is a pressing need to develop and organize bases of logistical support that can mobilize, support, and nurture activities that might develop into revolutionary struggles. Otherwise discontent can dissipate or become safety valves for systemic pressures — the blowing off of steam but little more. Uprisings and rebellions can be extended and given lengthier duration and more positively impactful outcomes.

Small groups cannot, despite the best wishes of insurrectionist, provoke mass uprisings or "manufacture revolution," or construct the conditions that will lead to mass rebellion. States and capital can sustain the effects of individual and disconnected acts of dissent or protest. They cannot tolerate the effects of class war (Johnson 2011, 309). We will again do well to recall John Gerassi's cautious notes with reference to the Black Panther Party and its strategies and tactics, as quoted previously. Failure reinforces conditioned pessimism. As Johnson suggests:

> And when we did dare to defy the odds (with total lack of coordinated unity and attention to strategy, tactics, and logistics), we were conditioned to believe (with some justification) that their reflex violence, their revenge, would be so brutal and widespread that the resulting suffering which our resistance provoked wasn't worth the effort. Therefore — failure leading to pessimism — any idea of waging a successful struggle for mass freedom was neutralized. (2011, 142–43)

In addition, the result of victories is that "their morale and desire to participate in resistance reach unforeseen heights" (Johnson 2011, 115). The need for preparation and reliable infrastructures is pressing. As Johnson suggests:

> Obviously, one cannot place blind confidence into a group of unconscious and disorganized people expecting them to be

able spontaneously to know how to solve complex economic, political, military, cultural and social problems, to know
what changes need to be made and to then pursue correct
methods of making those changes. This would be as ridicu-
lous as expecting a mass of people to spontaneously mobilize
an army and promptly defeat another well trained, supplied
and properly commanded army, while the former has no
strategic leadership who knew how to organize all relevant
factors — tactical, logistical and strategic — to weld that people into an effective fighting force. Leadership, guidance, organization, and discipline are imperative. (Johnson 2011, 231)

Shared infrastructures provide spaces and resources for shared
struggles and reinforce shared relationships. Infrastructures are
needed in the areas of shared life — workplaces, neighborhoods,
etc. Insurrectionary infrastructures provide experiments in pro-
ducing and living collectively beyond the state and capital.

When people of diverse social backgrounds work together to
identify, pursue, and secure our own aims and interests (rather
than the forced working together to meet the value needs of
capital as in the capitalist workplace) we can see that we share
interests with others among the exploited and oppressed and,
furthermore, that we have capacities for developing alternatives
on our own terms. Our interests and needs (food, shelter, clothing, health, education, pleasure, desire, love) are largely the same
and largely unmet under present state capitalist conditions.

CONCLUSION

Insurrectionists often bemoan the fact that movements are re-
cuperated before they become uprisings, their momentum lost
before they become full-blown uprisings. Yet these insurrectionists rarely figure out that the reason for this is not simply the
recuperative shenanigans of liberals and NGOs (though these
certainly do occur) but the lack of insurrectionary infrastruc-

tures that can provide the necessary scaffolding to maintain momentum, re-stoke fires, and sustain insurrectionary energies and impulses. It is this that can expand conflict into generalized revolt. It is these insurrectionary infrastructures that support insurrectionary forces and connect them with others engaged in such struggles in other conflicts.

The focus is too often on the liberal blankets that dampen insurrectionary fires rather than the insurrectionary infrastructures that can fuel them. At the same time the insurrectionists pose action itself, typically dramatic street outbursts, as an antidote to timidity which will spread like wildfire. It rarely plays out that way in the North American context.

As anarchist organizer James Herod suggests: "When it's all over, these insurrectionists will be showing up for work like always or standing again in the dole line. Nothing has changed. Nothing has been organized. No new associations have been created" (2007, 29). The impact to capital is minimal beyond perhaps the insurance premiums. As Herod asks: "What do capitalists care if they lose a whole city? They can afford it. All they have to do is cordon off the area of conflagration, wait for the fires to burn down, go in and arrest thousands of people at random, and then leave, letting the 'rioters' cope with their ruined neighborhoods as best they can" (2007, 29).

The notion that insurrections can spontaneously light a spark that will cause capitalism to catch fire for perhaps the final time is probably one that anarchist revolutionaries should shed. We might conclude with Herod who states unromantically: "Insurrections cannot destroy capitalism. I don't even think the ruling class is frightened of them anymore. You can rampage through the streets all you want, burn down your neighborhoods, and loot all the local stores to your heart's content. They know this will not go anywhere. They know that blind rage will burn itself out" (2007, 29).

There is a need to build and sustain infrastructures that can provide for sustained offensive, rather than reactive, struggle. As Herod suggests: "What is missing is free association, free assemblies, on the local level. If we added these into the mix, we would start getting somewhere. We could attack the ruling class on all fronts" (2007, 31). The aim is not to create an alternative that can be contained within the existing structures but rather to destabilize and destroy those structures.

REFERENCES

Johnson, Kevin "Rashid." 2011. *Defying the Tomb: Selected Prison Writing and Art of Kevin "Rashid" Johnson.* Montreal: Kersplebedeb.

Shantz, Jeff. 2012. *Green Syndicalism: An Alternative Red/Green Vision.* Syracuse: Syracuse University Press.

TO THE BARRICADES?

THE LIMITED INFRASTRUCTURES OF THE STREETS

5

PERHAPS THE GREAT image of insurrection (the best known insurrectionary infrastructure), one that inspires insurrectionists still today, is that of the barricade. Story images of Bakunin standing on the barricades at Paris and Dresden continue to stoke the romantic imagery of contemporary anarchists. Barricades played central parts in the uprisings of nineteenth century Europe and came to strike a lasting chord with writers and artists as well as insurgents. The heroic symbol of the barricade is associated with the Paris Commune despite their minimal use in that uprising.

The term barricade comes from the term *barriques* or barrels. Barrels filled with dirt to provide stability and solidity were central in the Day of the Barricades of May 12, 1588 in Paris. This provided the model for barricades to follow. Soldiers were stopped in their tracks. Among the barricades of insurrectionary and revolutionary legend and imagination are Petrograd 1917, Berlin 1919, Munich 1919, Barcelona 1936, Madrid 1937, Cairo 2011. The romantic connection with past glories was the impetus for the barricades of May 10, 1968 in Paris.

The barricade is an infrastructure of the moment, an ad hoc defense and base, forged as uprisings surge. They are no less than a matter of necessity of survival and escape if not offensive initiative. Using found objects of the streets (then carts, wagons, street stalls, now cars, trucks, garbage bins, newspaper boxes, always bricks and pavement stones) the barricade can grow quickly and spontaneously to provide an essential form of protection. And they can spread quickly, relatively easily. Even more, they can be effective — up to a point and for a time.

For Hazen, victorious barricades "are those that pin down the forces of repression, paralyze their movements and end up stifling them into impotence" (2013, ix). The historian though has to conclude though that the history of barricades "is only a succession of defeats" (2013, x). The victories, where there have been some, have been short lived and reversed. Notably, the French Revolution made only minimal use of the barricade.

Hazen suggests the barricade is not a regular retrenchment. Its special virtue he suggests "is to proliferate and form a network that crosses the space of the city," a "faculty of rapid multiplication" that can render the barricade an offensive tool (2013, ix). As Hazen reflects:

> Throughout the nineteenth century, the barricade was a *symbolic form of insurrection*: to unpave a street, overturn a cart, pile up furniture, is to give a signal, to show one's determination to fight, and fight together. Barricades form a network that links combatants together and lends unity to the struggle, even where it lacks a leader or overall plan. (2013, 123)

Yet this symbolic form offers little in the way of a model of self-defense against forces of a modern, mechanized state. Still it serves as the unspoken hope for defense of insurrectionists who would believe that a street battle can spark an uprising against states and capital.

THE HEYDAY OF THE BARRICADE

What historian Eric Hazen terms the "first proletarian barricades" were built by textile workers in Lyon in 1831 (2013, 53).

And, it must be noted, the workers were armed and able to take the also armed Lyon National Guard prisoner. When the army tried to assault the city they were foiled by barricades. Again, the neighbors rained rocks and tiles down on the soldiers' heads from the homes in the areas of the barricades. These were not simply street obstacles. Within a day the insurgents had taken the city of Lyon.

The insurgency was quickly defeated as lack of political vision and experiences in governing across industries and neighborhoods impeded consolidation of proletarian power (Hazen 2013, 57). The government by then had amassed the army at the city gates, and had the workers disarmed and key organizers arrested (Hazen 2013, 57). Thus the lesson of the need for experiences of federated governance prior to the uprising was highlighted very early on in the proletarian uprisings. It has been since, despite the hopefulness of insurrectionary desire. Notably too this is a lesson replayed later in other contexts such as general strikes where workers must take up many of the day to day provision and social service activities formerly directed by the government or business.

After the Lyon uprising, in fact, the proletariat set about building infrastructures of resistance in the city — organically realizing the need of social resources and the impact their lack had had in the defeat of the insurrection. The cooperative movement expanded as did social networks and radical working class newspapers. The result would be the development months later of a general strike in the city. An insurrection followed that resulted unfortunately in the routing of the proletariat. Still, a small number of workers, poorly armed, with no coordination or command wielded barricades to hold armies of 8,000 at bay for around a week.

In the 1848 insurrection in Paris, the people looted armories of the National Guard along with the building of barricades. This insurrection too showed the significance of the neighborhood and the use of armed defense as central to the uprising.

Bakunin himself describes events of February 24, shortly after his arrival from Belgium:

This enormous city, the centre of European culture, had suddenly become a wild Caucasus. In each street, almost everywhere, barricades erected like mountains and rising to the rooftops; above these barricades, between stones and damaged buildings, like Georgians on their rooftops, workers in blouses, black with powder and armed to the teeth [...]. And in the midst of this unbounded joy, this intoxication, all had become so gentle, so human, so pleasant, honest, modest, polite, kind and intelligent, that such a thing can be seen only in France, and even here only in Paris. (quoted in Hazen 2013, 73)

This was the start of the fire that would spread across Europe in 1848, a fire of which the *Communist Manifesto* was but one political product. Hazen notes, in any event, that the spark of Paris that became the "springtime of peoples" of 1848 fell on kindling that had already been well prepared (2013, 75). Among the notable insurrections was the uprising in Milan in March. There a unified population launched a stunning insurrection which saw sustained fighting over the course of five days. The roused inhabitants of the city were able to drive from the city the garrison of 13,000 commanded by none other than the vicious Austrian Field Marshal Radetzky (Ginsborg 2004, 11).

Demands were limited to those of national unity except in areas where radical networked resources had developed. In those areas calls for democratic freedoms and arming of the people were pressed (Hazen 2013, 76). Again the need for insurrectionary infrastructures is essential. Radical ideas do not emerge out of thin air because of an inspiring act. The notion of propaganda of the deed, and insurrections related to this, assumes sections of the public ready to "read" and understand and agree with the propaganda. And that occurs where spaces of discussion and debate have already been nurtured and such discussion and debate carried out. There must be a nurturing ground for radicalism to grow and thrive and take hold.

In case after case of insurrection the armies of absolutism withdrew before the insurgents without having been diminished. That would prove fatal. By the end of 1848 the absolutist order had been restored (Hazen 2013, 79).

Notably in the Dresden insurrection of 1849 none other than Bakunin would offer a grim assessment of the barricades as suitable infrastructures of insurrection. In the words of his friend Richard Wagner who also observed the insurrection:

> The Old Town of Dresden, with its barricades, was an interesting enough sight for the spectators. I looked on with amazement and disgust, but my attention was suddenly distracted by seeing Bakunin emerge from his hiding-place and wander among the barricades in a black frockcoat. But I was very much mistaken in thinking he would be pleased with what he saw; he recognized the childish inefficiency of all the measures that had been taken for defence, and declared that the only satisfaction he could feel in the state of affairs was that he need not trouble about the police, but could calmly consider the question of going elsewhere. (quoted in Hazen 2013, 81)

Wagner himself offered a less than glowing assessment of the insurrectionary sustainability of the barricade. In his words: "To persist in defending isolated barricaded streets in Dresden could, on the other hand, lend little but the character of an urban riot to the contest, although it was pursued with the highest courage" (quoted in Hazen 2013, 82). Thus one does not question the energy or commitment of the insurrectionists. But thy can not be sustained by hope and anger and courage alone, by the poetry of action. Insurrectionary infrastructures are needed.

February 1848 in Paris would mark the time of the last really victorious barricades (Hazen 2013, 85). As Hazen notes: "After that date, all urban battles in which the insurrection based its tactics on barricades would be defeated" (2013, 85). The character of urban fighting, and the resources available to the state in fighting urban battles had changed fundamentally. By this point with the development of artillery fire it was clear that such insurrections could only be defensive — momentarily and fatally.

Yet this is what contemporary insurrectionists would insti-
gate and view as some great strike against the system. Again, as
Auguste Blanqui reflected: "while the insurgents smoked their
pipes behind the paving-stones, the enemy successively concen-
trated all its forces on one point, then a second, a third, a fourth,
and in this way exterminated the insurrection piece by piece"
(quoted in Hazen 2013, 96).

After the June barricades were put down and insurgents mas-
sacred by at least 10,000, Blanqui offered this harsh assessment.
In his view:

> No point of leadership or overall command, not even consul-
> tation between the fighters. Each barricade has its particular
> group, more or less numerous but always isolated [...]. Often
> there is not even a leader to direct the defence. The fighters
> just do what they like. They remain, they leave, they return,
> as they see fit. At night they go home to sleep [...]. "Let each
> defend his post, and all will be well," the most solid ones say.
> This singular reasoning derives from the fact that the major-
> ity of insurgents fight in their own quarter, a capital error
> with disastrous consequences after defeat, especially in terms
> of denunciation by neighbours. For, with such a system de-
> feat is inevitable. (quoted in Hazen 2013, 95)

Note that Blanqui offers a view that is in opposition to much of
the opinion on barricades and locale. He does not argue for an
alternative approach and why it would be more effective.

The barricades of June 1848 were for Tocqueville not a political struggle but a class struggle — a "Servile War" in his terms, a
good term (quoted in Hazen 2013, 86). Tocqueville noted the co-
ordination that can emerge in such street battles. In his words:

> [T]he greatest and strangest that had ever taken place in our
> history, or perhaps in that of any other nation; the greatest
> because for four days more than a hundred thousand men
> took part in it, and there were five generals killed; the strang-
> est, because the insurgents were fighting without a battle cry,

leaders, or flag, and yet they showed wonderful powers of co-ordination and a military expertise that astonished the most experienced officers. (quoted in Hazen 2013, 85)

The barricade is remembered today as the symbol of the Paris Commune, which lasted seventy days between March 18 and May 28, 1871. Yet as historian Eric Hazen notes, the barricades only played a part in the last week of the Commune. It is less re-membered that Paris became isolated and targeted by Adolphe Thiers because the communes of Limoges, Marseilles, and Nar-bonne had all been put down within days.

One critical participant, Lefrançais, concluded that authori-tarian tendencies in the Commune led to its defeat, as centrali-zation worked against self-organizing for defense. In his words:

> The twenty-five years that have passed since then have only convinced me more that this minority [decentralist critics] were right, and that the proletariat will never succeed in truly emancipating itself without ridding itself of the Republic, the last form of authoritarian government, and by no means the least harmful. (quoted in Hazen 2013, 110, n. 2)

The defense did rally as the government forces entered Paris but by then it was certainly too late (Hazen 2013, 110). The defense had not been prepared and the necessary infrastructures for defense were absent or underdeveloped. Lefrançais notes that at one barricade there were cannons and machine guns but in eight weeks no one had even thought of cleaning them or both-ered to do the necessary work (Hazen 2013, 112).

THE NEED OF NEIGHBORHOODS

The barricade in its longer-term form emerges where there is a street, neighborhood, district way of life to defend and pre-existing networks, resources, and infrastructures to do so (Hazen 2013, x). That is where there are also some pre-existing connections, sentiments, worldviews; a strong conscience collective in Emile Durkheim's terms. As I have argued elsewhere, these shared worldviews require an ecosystem for growth and flourishing. These are precisely the incubators provided by infrastructures of resistance.

They involve street workers and neighborhood youth. These are aspects missing from protest insurrections which can be viewed as harms to street workers or local youth who will feel the impacts of retribution by police and the state more broadly. A political insurrection is not the same as a popular revolt.

Key in these earlier barricades though was support (munitions support) from neighboring houses and apartments as rocks and other items were thrown down on troops from windows and rooftops up above.

On the significance of connected neighborhoods with social relations and shared histories and interests, Hazen notes at length:

> Finally, the way in which cities are peopled has also changed. The traditional barricade was erected in a street by its own inhabitants, men, women and children, who also worked there or close by, and were ready to die there. With the capitalist organization of urban life, this street village has disappeared. Proletarians were compelled to work increasingly far from where they lived, and the site of struggle shifted to the factory, where it made no sense to pile up paving-stones. (2013, 126)

The large, open boulevards of the modern city are less suited to barricades than the narrow, meandering streets of old Europe (Hazen 2013, 125).

ON THE STREETS

Insurrection takes the streets as primary battlefields, a view that historian Eric Hazen suggests is as old as the cities themselves (2013, ix). Yet we must ask if this can still be said of the streets in the current period of long-range weapons controlled predominantly by advanced mechanized states. Air superiority too, at even basic levels like helicopters and drones as are currently deployed in major city centers like Surrey, British Columbia, raises further questions about the viability of the barricade and insurrections without infrastructures.

Yet there are even fewer resources currently available to contemporary insurrectionists in the current context of (dis)organizing and (dis)organization in North America other than the barricade. And most insurrectionary actions in those contexts are badly improvised and spontaneous (leading to a reliance on the hastily assembled barricade anyway).

I have seen directly and participated in this first hand in street battles ranging from the anti-globalization demonstrations against the World Bank and International Monetary Fund in Washington, DC in 2000 to the June 15 police riot in Toronto in 2001 to the 2001 Quebec City protests assaulted by tear gas and water cannons, to the 2010 mobilizations against the Olympics in Vancouver (as well as some smaller situations). Anyone who has been in these battles will be familiar with the scramble to topple and drag out dumpster bins, newspaper boxes, garbage cans, advertising boards, etc. simply to stop the advance of police.

Contemporary uprisings must obstruct and impede flows of energy and information and communication. Their sites are not streets but rail lines, docks, and logistical nodes. The means is not insurrection but sabotage, as I have written elsewhere (Shantz 2016).

REFERENCES

Ginsborg, Paul. 2004. *Silvio Berlusconi: Television, Power and Patrimony.* London: Verso.

Hazen, Eric. 2013. *A History of the Barricade.* London: Verso.

Shantz, Jeff. 2016. "Sabotage and the Flows of Capital: Communities Resist Assaults on Nature." *Fifth Estate* 395. https://theanarchistlibrary.org/library/jeff-shantz-sabotage-the-flows-of-capital.

6

PROTECT OURSELVES

ON THE NECESSITY OF SELF-DEFENSE

THOSE WHO STRUGGLE against states and capital must be prepared to defend themselves. To understand the nature of the state is to know that it will attack to kill when and where it feels a threat to its authority and power. Revolutionary mass struggle must be military as well as economic, political, and cultural. It must be mass-based. The absence of any of these factors leads to failure as the study of past revolutions suggests.

Even under the most brutal military powers of imperialism, resistance forces can succeed by building a secure base among the people (Johnson 2011, 30). This is achieved through the establishment of economic programs that serve the needs of the population. These programs are what I call infrastructures of resistance. They include schools, health clinics, food distribution centers, and so on. An example that Rashid Johnson gives is the work of Hamas. All of their work occurs in a small accessible space. The US and Canada are far more massive spaces, with areas less accessible to security forces yet with access to vast resources.

The working class and oppressed must develop united structures to coordinate their work and to bring together often isolated organizers. Economic, political, cultural, and military programs are needed that can displace the enemy (Johnson 2011, 31). Mass-based infrastructures are needed within the oppressed sections of the working class.

Resisting cultural domination, a favored preoccupation of much of the late-twentieth and early-twenty-first-century Left and alternative globalization movements, is no substitute for resisting economic, political, and military domination. Personal commitment is not enough. There is a need for shared ideas — for ideology. In the absence of such it is easy for people to lose the initiative to struggle. If action is based in a strong character or instigator, the momentum dissipates when that character is removed or transferred.

Since the election of Donald J. Trump as President of the United States of America there has been a renewed focus on issues of community self-defense, particularly among racialized oppressed communities, as the ones most targeted by the violence of the state and Rightwing vigilantes alike. There has also been a developing seriousness among the political Left, particularly among anarchist and antifascist, or antifa, activists.

COLLECTIVE SELF-DEFENSE

Typically in recent years when issues of self-defense have been raised in activist circles they have been posed on an individualist basis. So in anarchist free spaces or free schools going back to the 1990s at least there have been specific times dedicated for classes on personal self-defense and there have been trainings in martial arts or street smart self-defense. Some anarchist spaces have operated as dojos for a range of martial arts (judo, aikido, Brazilian jujitsu, etc.) on weekends or evenings.

In some areas antifa activists have started neighborhood watch groups against fascist, racist, white supremacist actions and as basic community defense in the wake of the Trumpist counter-revolution. In the 1980s and 1990s Anti-Racist Action groups, of which I was a participant, played similar roles in numerous cities and neighborhoods. At some point these could form the basis, with medics and health care workers, for replacements for state policing forces, on a basis of care and solidarity and mutual aid rather than punishment and repression.

Since the Trump election some groups have taken the individual self-defense in an armed direction, training in proper firearm usage and doing regular target practice. And it has long made sense for anarchists to do so. There will be no revolution, no matter how one conceptualizes it, without a need for antistatist and anti-capitalist forces to defend themselves with arms. More immediately it is almost certainly useful in a context in which much of the Right knows quite well how to use varieties of firearms. The disarming of the Left and progressive forces in the US has proven a disastrous outcome (and effect of the dominance of non-violent moralism).

These are all useful undertakings and will likely be necessary and essential in a period of rising Rightwing, even proto-fascist, violence and nationalist assault. One might well need to defend oneself from personal assault by a neo-Nazi or white supremacist. Or one might simply want to know proper technique in the event of an opportunity to punch a Nazi.

And, more to the point, there are real and legitimate traditions of community self-defense including armed self-defense, among exploited and oppressed communities. One need only reference the Black Panther Party and Robert F. Williams and the Black Armed Guard. It is long forgotten that the Social Democratic Party in Austria had a massive armed wing, the Austrian Schutzbund, among the largest working class militias on the planet in the 1930s (which was unfortunately demobilized by the party right as the Nazi threat grew). These should be models for contemporary organizing in the present period. Williams's 1962 book *Negroes with Guns* should be required reading in the present period (while recognizing its patriarchal missteps and limitations). Notably Williams relied on large numbers of Black military veterans, a possible signal for contemporary organizers. It is long forgotten among so-called pacifists and non-violence fundamentalists that Rosa Parks delivered the eulogy at Williams's funeral in 1996.

Yet these example show that self-defense requires even more resources and infrastructures to support resistance against more than personal or group assaults. There is a need for resource centers and provisions. There is a need for health care and medical supplies and care givers. "Where are the anarchist doctors and nurses," remains an important question. There is a need for safe houses and safe house networks.

There is a need for quick strike defense in support of communities under attack. That is the capacity to move enough workers to shut down strategic workplaces in support of community defense (the workplaces will be site specific depending on the city, town, etc., and local economies and geographies). There will also be a need to mobilize neighborhoods to provide support and cover in situations of assault. This could also include neighborhood strikes (rent strikes, consumption strikes, etc.) or strategic acts of disobedience and disruption (looting a grocery store, takeover of a gas station, etc.).

DESIRE ARMED

It is virtually impossible to defeat state capital through armed assault. There is no way for the working classes to assume the level of firepower controlled by governments, large and small. Neither should they want it. It is a massive waste of human and natural resources and materials. It also serves to structure social relations as hierarchical and authoritarian. At the same time armed defense will be necessary.

Guerrilla warfare, as part of a strategy of assuming state power through force of arms will not work. It is a failed strategy the results of which would be the continuation of state power. It is an approach based on the mistaken assumption that capital and states will not kill civilian populations to get to the guerrillas. Recent history shows, on the contrary, that they will pursue such a policy without hesitation or regret. Statist militaries will occupy territory, displace people, and deploy violence against entire communities as the wars in Iraq and Afghanistan show.

Still some romantic youth want to bring this strategy into the belly of the beast. Such was also the temptation within the faltering movements of the late 1960s and early 1970s. It has not surprisingly this has emerged as a proposed option as the Occupy movements dissipated and were put down. That would prove disastrous. The states in liberal democracies have massive firepower matched with new techniques of surveillance and repression. Such an approach does not bear the new world within it (Herod 2007, 25). Instead, it offers capital a new way of to demonize and fear monger against emergent radical movements — to portray anarchists as terrorists all over again.

Infrastructures will need to be defended and armed struggle will likely be necessary and effective in specific contexts. Such was certainly true in recent mass struggles such as the occupations of Tahrir Square during the Egyptian Spring. The point is that other methods and strategies will need to form the primary basis for anti-capitalist resistance and social transformation. In any event, social movements in North America are a long ways away from posing the sort of threat to states or capital that would pose the question of meaningful armed struggle.

A fundamental commitment to nonviolence as an unwavering principle should in no way be inferred from this. Nonviolence is a tactical and practical dead end. As Herod suggests:

> Nonviolence is a key ideological weapon of a violent ruling class. This class uses it to pacify us; it uses its mass media to preach nonviolence incessantly. Such rhetoric is an effective weapon because we all (but they don't) want to live in a peaceful world. We would do well to chart a careful course through this swamp. (2007, 5)

Such is true of tactics based on nonviolence such as non-violent civil disobedience. The assessment of protests offered by anarchist organizer James Herod is instructive. For Herod:

Acts of civil disobedience cannot destroy capitalism. They can sometimes make strong moral statements. But moral statements are pointless against immoral persons. They fall on deaf ears. Therefore, the act of deliberately breaking a law and getting arrested is of limited value in actually breaking the power of the rulers. (2007, 29)

Overcoming states and capital will by definition involve violence. And there will be a need for seriously organized collective self-defense on various levels.

REPRESSION

For political prisoner Rashid Johnson, "mass involvement or sympathy with organized tactical armed resistance is the one form of struggle that truly endangers empire's power" (2011, 293). Infrastructures of resistance provide a logistical base for building mass support. Many of these infrastructures were destroyed and/or demobilized following the state repression against the upsurge of the late 1960s and early 1970s. There will be dedicated efforts by states and capital to isolate the armed front from the masses.

The "war on crime" played a part in this. In the 1960s and 1970s, Daniel Patrick Moynihan advised the Nixon administration to achieve this goal partly by criminalizing the image of the armed front. As today, revolutionary activity became constructed as terrorism. Concerted efforts were also put into dissolving the lower strata grassroots support and replacing it with middle class social conformity and moralism. The "war on crime" initiated first under Nixon, was directed at stopping the spread of organized armed resistance and the militant tactics of working class and poor youth, particularly Black youth.

Under NSC 46 the government explicitly stated that continued growth of Black struggles for economic justice in the 1970s would require violent repression from the government to stabilize the social relations of working class and poor communities. NSC 46 noted that such steps would be "misunderstood" both inside and outside the US and could lead to further trouble for the administration (Johnson 2011, 314). Middle strata elites, with interests in access to and maintenance of capitalist markets, undermine and eventually replace working class and poor people among the grassroots leadership.

Revolutionary activities and armed struggle tactics are demonized and degraded. Existing institutions are presented as means for meeting social needs and energies are channeled toward statist or market based institutions and practices. As Johnson notes:

> The ensuing mass incarceration, criminalization, concentration of police and surveillance, and the vast Prison-Industrial Complex targeted especially at poor, urban Blacks, has been a conscious tactical response of empire to repress anti-colonial, anti-capitalist, and revolutionary fervor amongst the oppressed classes. (2011, 298–99)

NOT PARTY TIME: ON WRONG CONCLUSIONS

Sectarian socialist groupings, like the Socialist Workers Party (UK), International Socialists (Canada), or International Socialist Organization (US), have long argued that the failure of uprisings like the Paris Commune or Hungarian uprising suggests the need for a centralized party to coordinate resistance and move to an offensive. This is not the conclusion to draw. It is rather an extreme case of confirmation bias. They are party builders who want a part so they see in each failing the absence of a party and the need for one in the future.

The argument to be drawn is not for a party to manage the people. Rather these cases and others speak to a range of issues, including the need for self-organizing and self-determining experiences ahead of an uprising. They also speak to needed shifts in morality and inhibitions, over violence or respect for authority for example). At the very least it speaks to the need to break the hegemony of non-violence and pacifism that restrains resistance and leads to second guessing and a lack of self-confidence. A party is irrelevant — a distraction — except in the possibility of developing counter-hegemonic perspectives and offering some shared resources (including arms and munitions, but none of the sectarian groupings are organizing these). The need is for insurrectionary infrastructures with some practice and experience and coordinated through interlinked (federated if you will) assemblies in workplaces and neighborhoods.

Insurrectionary infrastructures include solidarity economies to provide support to communities on a non-monetary, non-charitable basis. These are economies of solidarity and mutual aid. These might be based in self-managed workplaces. They can of course include materials and equipment liberated from exploitative workplaces. Another reason to build solid workplace, working class networks in a range of work sites.

MASS OR ACTIVIST?

This is by no means a suggestions that oppressed or exploited groups or communities should wait to rebel or not rise up whenever they determine it is necessary or are impelled by circumstances to do so. Not at all. *Mass* uprisings can and do move things along very quickly, changing circumstances and probabilities. They can and do change the learning curve.

The suggestion here is rather that activist insurrections, street battles, aggressive protests, vandalism, etc. are not mass or popular uprisings and should not be mistaken for them. Neither do they have the same impacts on social outcomes. Even more, they do not hold the same potential for social change, resistance, revolution. Their impacts can be largely negative — leading to increased repression (of communities and groups not even involved), misunderstanding, contempt from oppressed and exploited people (who may be put back by or bear the brunt of responses to such activist actions).

At the same time, it can also be said that in any event both activist insurrections and mass uprisings stand better chances of survival, sustenance, expansion, or success where there are substantial resources and infrastructures to support and defend them. And defense will *always* be necessary during and after insurrections, uprisings — even aggressive protests. There is no getting around that basic fact.

The idea that an activist insurrection or aggressive protest will be the spark that lights a prairie fire or an act of propaganda of the deed to spur rebellion further has not borne out. This formulation is the anarchist version of the outside agitator thesis favored by conservatives.

Not all acts of outrage against the everyday insults and injuries of capitalist society (breaking a store window, burning a cop car, etc.) are the same either in impact or consequence and they do not stand as necessarily insurrectionary acts — though I might very much enjoy each and every one of them on a personal level (and would never counsel anyone against setting any cop property ablaze — ever).

There is a meaningful difference in both the character, intensity, and relevance between a Black neighborhood in Detroit, Ferguson, or Los Angeles rising up against any instance of police violence and systemic racism and anarchist insurrectionists attacking symbols of consumer culture during a student protest or anti-Olympics demonstration. A black bloc is not a Black uprising.

THERE WILL BE BLOOD

In any event, it should never be lost sight of that insurrectionist and non-insurrectionist anarchists are anarchists and as such desire and seek the abolition of the state and capital. That means by definition that there is a recognition that fundamental, essential, social change will involve some level of violence — no state has ever abolished itself voluntarily — and there will always be a necessity for self defense among groups seeking social change who will be targeted (as they already are) for violence by the state.

The goal of all anarchism is not to eliminate violence in social struggle (a futile and impossible pursuit given the nature of the state) but to limit the amount, degree, and extent of violence and harm inflicted by state agents, and their vigilante supporters, on the poor, oppressed, and exploited. And this is part of the emphasis on insurrectionary infrastructures. Non-material (emotional) and material resources and spaces are necessary bit to defend communities and workplaces under attack but also to organize possible, and necessary, offensives.

REFERENCES

Herod, James. 2007. *Getting Free: Creating and Association of Democratic Autonomous Neighborhoods.* Boston: Lucy Parsons Center.

Johnson, Kevin "Rashid." 2011. *Defying the Tomb: Selected Prison Writing and Art of Kevin "Rashid" Johnson.* Montreal: Kersplebedeb.

7

INSURRECTIONARY INFRASTRUCTURES

BASES FOR OFFENSE AND DEFENSE

ANARCHISTS RECOGNIZE THAT struggles for a better world beyond state capitalism must occur on two simultaneous levels. They must be capable of defeating states and capital and they must, at the same time, provide infrastructures or foundations of the future society in the present day. Indeed, this latter process will be a fundamental part of the work of defeating states and capital.

Through infrastructures of resistance movements will build alternatives but, as importantly, have capacities to defend the new social formations. These infrastructures of resistance will directly confront state capitalist power. Thus they will need to be defended from often savage attack.

The key impulse is to shift the terrain of anti-capitalist struggle from a defensive position — reacting to elite policies and practices or merely offering dissent — to an offensive one — contesting ruling structures and offering workable alternatives. Movements need to shift from a position of resistance to one of active transformation. Anarchist James Herod encourages anarchists to take the initiative in building new social relations rather than simply resisting the offenses of states and capital. Anarchists need to busy themselves with offensive strategies rather than defensive maneuvers (which make up most of undertakings of activists).

Anarchist revolutionaries must radically shift the terrain of anti-capitalist struggles, moving to new battlegrounds rather than staying in the streets of protest and the town squares of Occupy movements. For Herod and other constructive anarchists there are three primary sites of struggle with which anarchists must be engaged. These are the neighborhoods, workplaces, and households.

Successful organizing in these areas should provide means to defeat states and capital, while also making the new world in the present — rather than waiting for a post-capitalist future. This shift must involve offensive as well as defensive strategies.

Movements have been oriented for too long toward reactive or defensive actions. They have also become predominantly oppositional. They can mobilize to speak out against or oppose specific state or corporate practices, or the challenge rotten pieces of legislation. They do not offer inspiring, and real, material visions for the future. Or even provide a serious glimpse into a new world in the making. They do not take the offensive, push the envelope, set the agenda (or put up new ones) very often. This is true of much movement activity in the Global North. And people who desire, and desperately need, change are not drawn to the rote ritualism that much of oppositional politics has become.

And it is more than this. The ritualism of oppositional politics does not really pose much opposition at all anyway. They do not challenge structures of inequality, oppression, or exploitation. They do not make powerholders tremble. They even have negative effects in discouraging people while buttressing false notions of participation and respect for dissent within liberal democratic mythologizing. So we must question the amount of work and resources that movements put into street protests and other largely symbolic actions like Occupy, for example.

Former right-wing Premier of Ontario, Mike Harris, who faced mass demonstrations and symbolic strikes, famously remarked contemptuously, in the face of mass street demonstrations: "I don't do protests." Yet spectacular events like demonstrations, protests, and public occupations dominate activist imaginations and organizational visions. This demonstration fixation has hindered social movements in liberal democracies for generations. As Herod reminds us:

> This predilection for protests and demonstrations prevailed throughout the 1960s, as the movements travelled to Washington, DC, time and again, taking to the streets. We are still like children, only able to "raise a ruckus." We are not yet adults who can assemble, reason together, take stock of our options, devise a strategy, and then strike, to both defeat our enemies and build the world we want. (2007, 3)

Herod notes that most of the dominant strategies deployed by social movements have not advanced us very far toward the goal of abolishing capitalism. Mainstream approaches to politics — particularly those of liberal parties and social democracy continue to hold out the false promise of a painless reformatting of the current social system and achievement of social progress through compromise with elites toward gradual reforms.

Some approaches — such as Leninist vanguard parties, social-democratic electoralism, and guerrilla warfare — should be abandoned. That much should be clear from the examples of more than 150 years of experience globally. Others, such as strikes, insurrections, and occupations should be organized as part of broader strategies for developing free associations in workplaces, neighborhoods, and households — all aimed at a broader social reconstruction.

BREAKING HEGEMONY
THROUGH SELF-ACTIVITY

Capital and states control massive resources for the shaping and framing of public opinion, sentiment, and values. Beyond mass media, television, radios, computers, newspapers, and video games, there is schooling, electoral systems, corporate domination of culture, and workplace messaging.

A society dominated by so-called, and often self-appointed, authorities and experts tends to make people suspicious of their own capacities for decision making. This is an effect of the power of administrative bureaucracies that have spread into virtually all spheres of social life. People become conditioned to defer to authorities or turn to experts for even personal decisions. From talk shows to self-help literature the proliferation of experts has become extensive especially under neoliberal regimes of self-discipline and self-regulation. This is a form of governance in which we are expected to surveil ourselves according to professional algorithms and ideations.

I have suggested that logistics determines strategy. This is what building insurrectionary infrastructures is about. It prepares needed logistical capacity and opens new possibilities for action against and hopefully one day beyond states and capital. As mentioned previously, Sun Tzu suggested that battles are won or lost before they are even fought. Organization and preparation do indeed remain key.

Recently there have emerged a variety of experiments with alternative forms of social and economic organization, as part of broader struggles against capitalist globalization. These experiments provide alternatives to capitalist economic rationality, if only in embryonic form (Shorthose 2000). The movements against capitalist globalization, the affinity-based organizations they have developed and their emphasis on self-valorizing activities, suggest not only an opposition to global capital's economic rationality and its statist supports, but also suggests a yearning for economic, social, and political alternatives to that rationality.

These experiments go beyond the ephemeral manifestations of protest politics to begin the work of putting forward an alternative infrastructure, both for the day-to-day necessities of sustaining movements in struggle as well as to provide a space for developing social, economic, and political relationships that prefigure the sorts of relationships that people would like to see replace those that characterize those of contemporary capitalism.

Shorthose (2000, 191) suggests that these "micro-experiments" present "the potential for a more convivial and sustainable future as well as empowering individuals to maintain a greater sense of economic security and an expanded sphere of autonomy away from the vagaries of the market." Micro-experiments which come from this imaginative attitude try to expand the real democratic control that people have over their economic and social lives, and allow them to expand their creativity and self-determination" (Shorthose 2000, 192). Gorz (1983) suggests that what is needed is not a new coherent political scheme but instead opportunities to develop capacities to change the logic of social development.

One notable example of the speed and breadth of development of oppositional resources is the quick rise of independent media networks after the Seattle protests against the WTO in 1999. Independent news and discussion sites sprang up globally and gave rise to a range of alternative media ventures in numerous local contexts. Some of these include: Indymedia, rabble.ca, resist.ca, and riseup.net.

A new social world cannot be built from scratch. Nor does it need to be. The mutual aid relationships and already existing associations that people have organized around work and personal interests (clubs, groups, informal workplace networks, even subcultures) can provide possible resources. At the same time, many infrastructures are needed, even today, in working class and poor neighborhoods and households and many workers have only loose informal connections in their workplaces.

Apartment complexes hold many possibilities. They already bring large numbers of working class and oppressed people together in close proximity and in important spaces of living. They can organize through direct assemblies to work up their shared resources. These include cooking, maintenance, laundry, health care, education, birthing rooms, and recreational facilities (Herod 2007, 11). We have seen examples of these efforts in emerging tenants' rights organizing and in the successful rent strikes carried out in high rise apartments my old neighborhood of Parkdale in Toronto.

NEIGHBORHOOD ASSEMBLIES

Assemblies are gatherings in which people participate directly in the community-specific decisions that govern their social lives (Herod 2007, ix). Giving participatory decision-making a central place will distinguish new social relations from the archic, or authoritarian, relations that currently dominate within state capitalist societies. The face-to-face decision-making assembly is the basic unit for reorganizing social life beyond the household. Larger associations are rooted in or based on this core social unit (Herod 2007, x).

Autonomous relations will be self-governing but not quite self-sufficient. It is not a situation of autarky. There will be intercourse among and between different units. There will be gift giving and swaps and sharing of resources in various ways.

Capitalist power relies on conditions of anonymity and isolation. This fact has been recognized by sociologists such as Ferdinand Tönnies and Robert Park. Even conservative theorists such as Emile Durkheim were attuned to this key feature of the organic solidarity of capitalist divisions of labor.

Most cities, and the neighborhoods that make them up, lack assembly and meeting spaces where residents can come together, discuss, debate, and make the decisions over fundamental matters that affect their lives. This is an architectural representation of the lack of real democracy, and public intercourse, in capitalist societies — the absence of an agora.

RANK-AND-FILE ORGANIZING AND THE WILDCAT

Similarly general strikes cannot have a meaningful impact in the absence of infrastructures of resistance. As Herod notes:

General strikes cannot destroy capitalism. There is an upper limit of about six weeks as to how long they can even last. Beyond that society starts to disintegrate. But since the general strikers have not even thought about reconstituting society through alternative social arrangements, let alone created them, they are compelled to go back to their jobs just to survive, to keep from starving. All a government has to do is wait them out, perhaps making a few concessions to placate the masses. This is what Charles de Gaulle did in France in 1968. (2007, 27)

Essential services must be maintained under general strike conditions. In the absence of alternative associations or capacities to run workplaces to meet our social needs, water, energy, food, and medical services would not be available. The strike would not last long on that basis. Strikes require pre-existing infrastructures and logistical capacities. The workplace organizing that can contribute to meaningful social strike action includes rank and file alternatives, such as flying squads, working groups, and direct action groups.

The insurrectionary form of the labor strike is the wildcat strike. The wildcat is the strike without permissions. It is the illegal strike in a period of legalized (and tamed) unions, with legal constraints, under strike conditions that have been limited by law. The wildcat expresses the insurgent needs and desires of workers in overcoming their limited positions as workers — becoming fully human in asserting needs beyond those of a collective agreement with the boss or a joint labor-management committee or formally recognized grievance process.

The wildcat rises against bosses and union bureaucrats and contract managers alike. It is a movement of workers from below. Self-determined and self-determining. The wildcat puts the needs of workers above the requirements of law and the collective agreement because it is a rising of workers themselves. The wildcat also challenges fundamentally the capital–labor relationship as it does not accept the rights of bosses and claims of ownership to in any way control or delimit the actions of workers and their labor (through collective agreements, contracts, legal frameworks, etc.).

ON INSURRECTIONARY INFRASTRUCTURES

There is a pressing need to take decision-making out of government bureaucracies, parliament, and corporate suites and boardrooms and relocate it in autonomous assemblies of working class and poor people. There is also a need to take activism out of the atypical realms of demonstrations and protests and root it in everyday contexts and the daily experiences of working class and poor people's social lives.

This would serve to meet practical needs — of shelter, education, health, and wellbeing — while also raising visions for broader alternatives and stoking the capacity to imagine or see new possibilities. Building infrastructures of resistance will directly affect movements in practical and visionary ways. It will also challenge ruling elites by pushing them into reactive, rather than purely offensive, and confident, positions. Such infrastructures of resistance would shift possibilities for strategizing and mobilization. They might render demonstrations unnecessary. As Herod suggests:

> If we had reorganized ourselves into neighborhood, workplace, and household assemblies, and were struggling to seize power there, then we would have a base from which to stop ruling-class offensives like neoliberalism. If we then chose to demonstrate in the streets, there would be some teeth to it, rather than it being just an isolated ephemeral event, which can be pretty much ignored by our rulers. We would not be just protesting but countering. We have to organize ourselves in such a way that we have the power to counter them, not just protest against them, to refuse them to neutralize them. This cannot be done by affinity groups, nongovernmental organizations (NGOs), or isolated individuals converging peri-

odically at world summits to protest against the ruling class, but only by free associations rooted in normal everyday life. (2007, 2–3)

Transformation must focus on controlling means of reproduction as well as means of production. Focus on workers control alone leaves communities unable to allocate resources effectively and efficiently to meet broader needs (social or ecological). At the same time, community control without control of means of production would be futile, a fantasy. Even more, leaving households as privatized realms would reinforce an unequal gender division of labor and reinforce the duality of public and private realms of which anarchists generally critical (Herod 2007, 13). At the very least, neighborhood assemblies will constantly lose people who need to move in search of employment in the absence of worker control of industry.

Building infrastructures of resistance encourages novel ways of thinking about revolutionary transformation. Rather than the familiar form of street organization or protest action, within constructive anarchist approaches, the action is in the organizing. As Herod suggests:

This is the way to think of the revolution. It is a people reassembling themselves (reordering, reconstituting, and reorganizing themselves) into free associations at home, at work, and in the neighborhood. Capitalists will fight this. They may outlaw the meetings, bust them up by force, arrest those attending, or even murder those in attendance. But if we are determined, they will not be able to block us from reconstituting ourselves into the kind of social world we want. (2007, 16)

There need to be already existing infrastructures or else a radical or revolutionary transformation will be impossible (or disastrous). On the need for pre-existing revolutionary infrastructures, we might concur with Herod who suggests:

Workplace associations would have to be permanent assemblies, with years of experience under their belts, before they could have a chance of success. They cannot be new forms suddenly thrown up in the depths of a crisis or the middle of a general strike, with a strong government still waiting in the wings, supported by its fully operational military forces. (2007, 26)

Infrastructures of resistance can help to root people in particular communities and local struggles against states and capital and for new arrangements, rather than in ephemeral, single issue campaigns. This can be a significant advance and lead to further successes. As Herod notes:

Many millions of us, though, are rootless and quite alienated from a particular place or local community. We are part of the vast mass of atomized individuals brought into being by the market for commodified labor. Our political activities tend to reflect this. We tend to act as free-floating protesters. But we could start to change this. We could begin to root ourselves in our local communities. (2007, 31)

The construction of infrastructures of resistance will give durability to as well as allow for an otherwise unattainable breadth of action for specific campaigns, providing increased opportunities to link up and generalize struggles. For Herod: "Yet many of us could start establishing free associations at work, at home, and in the neighborhood. In this way, our fights to stop what we don't like through single-issue campaigns could be combined with what we do want. Plus, we would have a lot more power to stop what we don't like. Our single-issue campaigns might prove to be more successful" (2007, 31).

Insurrections will certainly be necessary, even inevitable, parts of radical social transformation. But in the absence of infrastructures of resistance within communities of the working classes and oppressed, to contextualize, support, and defend such actions (both materially and morally) they are little more than safety valves allowing people to blow off some steam and release some anger (valuable in its own right to be sure but not advancing revolutionary aims) — with high costs involved.

In recent contexts in which uprisings have been impactful, as in Greece, supportive infrastructures in communities, specific neighborhoods in particular, give even limited insurrections greater meaning and power.

SYMBOLS OF FUTILITY

Symbolic protests and civil disobedience are politics of the powerless or those who feel outrage at social conditions but lack alternatives when confronted with state capitalist power. As Herod suggests:

> But they are basically the actions of powerless persons. Powerless individuals must use whatever tactics they can, of course. But that is the point. Why remain powerless, when by adopting a different strategy (building strategic associations) we could become powerful, and not be reduced to impotent acts like civil disobedience against laws we had no say in making and that we regard as unjust? (2007, 29–30)

Protests, even mass demonstrations, are largely about shaming those who have no shame. Symbolic actions attempt to pose moral accusations against those who view such accusations as irrelevant. Such actions are virtually meaningless. They pose no real challenge to power-holders. Their sole impact, and the limit of their accomplishment, is restricted to the possible achievement of awareness raising. That is if people pay any attention to them. Such actions are dependent on mass media and leave the message of participants in the hands of corporate media that have no reason to be sympathetic to the movement or its message (or to even understand or accurately report them).

Demonstrations have become like religious rituals for social movements. They are the most common form of organizing action despite being one of the least effective. As Herod outlines:

> As a rule, demonstrations barely even embarrass capitalists, let alone frighten or damage them. Demonstrations are just a form of petition usually. They petition the ruling class regarding some grievance, essentially begging it to change its policies. They are not designed to take any power or wealth away from capitalists. Demonstrations only last a few hours or days and then, with rare exception, everything goes back to the way it was. If demonstrations do win an occasional concession, it is usually minor and short-lived. They do not build an alternative social world. Rather, they mostly just alert the ruling class that it needs to retool or invent new measures to counter an emerging source of opposition. (2007, 32)

Even more though demonstrations are a rather substantial drain on already limited labor, energy, and resources of organizing groups. They take time away from other more pressing but difficult tasks.

Beyond these considerations, symbolic demonstrations and protests give organizers a false sense of achievement and misleading sense of relevance. One thousand people at a demonstration is viewed as a success for organizers when, in fact, the real impact of such actions on economic and political elites and power-holders is minimal or non-existent. One might well argue that activists could cease holding demonstrations altogether with little or no impact on real world organizing and struggles against states and capital. As Herod identifies:

> Our opposition has no teeth. In order to give some bite to our protests we would have to reorganize ourselves, reorient ourselves, by rooting ourselves assembling ourselves on the local level. Then when we went off on demonstrations to protest ruling-class initiatives and projects there would be some strength behind the protests, rather than just shouted slo-

gans, unfurled banners, hoisted placards, street scuffles, and clever puppets. We would be in a position to take action if our demands were not met. Then when we chanted, "Whose Streets? Our Streets!" our words might represent more than just a pipe dream. (2007, 32)

For all of the time and energy put into organizing, participating in, and debriefing after demonstrations, relatively little is directed towards infrastructures of resistance. The balance in this regard needs to change if movements are to move from dissent to petition to mobilize a counter-power to states and capital. As Herod proposes:

Rather than taking to the streets and marching off all the time, protesting this or that (while the police take our pictures), we would be better off staying at home and building up our workplace, neighborhood, and household associations until they are powerful enough to strike at the heart of capitalism. We cannot build a new social world in the streets. (2007, 33)

One important infrastructural development involves new decision-making arrangements. That is the real power and significance of the Occupy mobilizations and the real, pressing message of anarchist currents within them.

This makes them potentially more effective than regular demonstrations and insurrections, and even acts of direct action such as boycotts and sabotage. The extent to which they impel new decision making processes and provide means to extend these processes to other spheres of action, the Occupy-inspired movements will have made a significant transformation in organizing against states and capital and for new social relations.

A NOTE ON REPRODUCTIVE LABOR

The preference for insurrection over infrastructures in some insurrectionist perspectives is perhaps related to the broader patriarchal and sexist biases in organizing more broadly. The flash street action has long been prioritized as domain of healthy energetic males. Less romanticized has been the mundane work of everyday reproduction and care giving and provision which has too often been undertaken by or bottom-lined by women-identified people in the movement.

Street battles are exciting, lively, thrilling, risky. They release adrenaline and positive endorphins. The everyday work of infrastructure building can be trying, tiring, and, sure, even boring. It has those moments.

While insurrectionists refer to the politics of everyday organizing as boring and romanticize the thrill of action they are in part saying people's everyday lives and need fulfillment are boring (dismissive and paternalistic) and overlooking the great work that is done to sustain and prepare the moments of action (and care for people afterward).

And make no mistake this is often a gendered division of interests and activities within movements and projects. Sustaining work is also action though and we should not forget this. This is not to say that there is a uniform gendered split in activist work. And indeed every insurrectionary and revolutionary movement has seen streets filled with women kicking ass. Anyone and everyone can enjoy a street battle in various ways. Rather it is to say that everyday work in activist circles is disproportionately undertaken by people identifying as women.

CONCLUSION

For many anarchist organizers "[d]estroying capitalism is more a matter of rearranging ourselves socially (reconstructing our

social relations) than of propagating a particular set of ideas"
(Herod 2007, 36). Rather than engaging in propaganda work,
the pressing need is to meet with neighbors and co-workers to
form associations from which effective and durable organizing
might be carried out.

Anarchists have always sought organizational alternatives to
the institutions of states and capital. As Herod suggests:

> Anarchists have always called for worker and peasant self-
> managed cooperatives. The long term goals have always been
> clear: to abolish wage slavery, eradicate a social order orga-
> nized solely around the accumulation of capital for its own
> sake, and establish in its place a society of free people who
> democratically and cooperatively self-determine the shape of
> their social world. (2007, 40)

Anarchist goals necessarily require concrete means to pursue
and achieve them. These means involve new social arrangements and associations and new organizational forms. Herod
suggests that the constructive anarchist approach is one of hol-
lowing out or, in his words, gutting capitalism. This is not a full
on frontal attack aimed at seizing the state or overthrowing the
system in a moment of insurrectionary rupture or revolution.

It is, however, an aggressive and militant strategy. It is based
on developing alternatives and resources that can provide for
options beyond state capitalist institutions. Thus there is a
positive and creative — a constructive — foundation to this approach. This is a distinctive approach to revolutionary social
transformation. As Herod proposes:

> This is how it has to be done. This is a plausible, realistic strat-
> egy. To think that we could create a whole new world of de-
> cent social arrangements overnight, in the midst of a crisis,
> during a so-called revolution or the collapse of capitalism, is
> foolhardy. Our new social world must grow within the old,
> and in opposition to it, until it is strong enough to dismantle
> and abolish capitalist relations. Such a revolution will never

happen automatically, blindly, determinably, because of the inexorable materialist laws of history. It will happen, and only happen, because we want it to, and because we know what we're doing and how we want to live, what obstacles have to be overcome before we can live that way, and how to distinguish between our social patterns and theirs. (2007, 38–39)

This is decidedly not about dropping out. It is not about seeking to escape capital to live in an imaginary elsewhere — in a commune or subculture. It is about acts of refusal. It will need to involve the refusal of work for wages. It will also need to be defended against repression and coercion. Insurrection requires infrastructures.

REFERENCES

Gerassi, John. 1971. *The Coming of the New International: A Revolutionary Anthology.* New York: The World Publishing Company.

Herod, James. 2007. *Getting Free: Creating and Association of Democratic Autonomous Neighborhoods.* Boston: Lucy Parsons Center.

Shorthose, James. 2000. "Micro-Experiments in Alternatives." *Capital and Class* 72: 191–207.